Safety Management Systems
Complete Self-Assessment Guide

The guidance in this Self-Assessment is based on Safety Management Systems best practices and standards in business process architecture, design and quality management. The guidance is also based on the professional judgment of the individual collaborators listed in the Acknowledgments.

Notice of rights

You are licensed to use the Self-Assessment contents in your presentations and materials for internal use and customers without asking us - we are here to help.

Trademarks

Table of Contents

About The Art of Service   8

Included Resources - how to access   8
Purpose of this Self-Assessment   10
How to use the Self-Assessment   11
Safety Management Systems
Scorecard Example   13

Safety Management Systems
Scorecard   14

BEGINNING OF THE
SELF-ASSESSMENT: 15
CRITERION #1: RECOGNIZE   16

CRITERION #2: DEFINE: 28

CRITERION #3: MEASURE: 44

CRITERION #4: ANALYZE: 58

CRITERION #5: IMPROVE: 74

CRITERION #6: CONTROL: 90

CRITERION #7: SUSTAIN: 103
Safety Management Systems and Managing Projects,
Criteria for Project Managers: 128
1.0 Initiating Process Group: Safety Management Systems
                                                          129

1.1 Project Charter: Safety Management Systems   132

1.2 Stakeholder Register: Safety Management Systems   134

1.3 Stakeholder Analysis Matrix: Safety Management Systems   135

2.0 Planning Process Group: Safety Management Systems   137

2.1 Project Management Plan: Safety Management Systems   139

2.2 Scope Management Plan: Safety Management Systems   141

2.3 Requirements Management Plan: Safety Management Systems   143

2.4 Requirements Documentation: Safety Management Systems   145

2.5 Requirements Traceability Matrix: Safety Management Systems   147

2.6 Project Scope Statement: Safety Management Systems   149

2.7 Assumption and Constraint Log: Safety Management Systems   151

2.8 Work Breakdown Structure: Safety Management Systems   153

2.9 WBS Dictionary: Safety Management Systems   155

2.10 Schedule Management Plan: Safety Management Systems   158

2.11 Activity List: Safety Management Systems   160

2.12 Activity Attributes: Safety Management Systems   162

2.13 Milestone List: Safety Management Systems   164

2.14 Network Diagram: Safety Management Systems   166

2.15 Activity Resource Requirements: Safety Management
Systems   168

2.16 Resource Breakdown Structure: Safety Management
Systems   170

2.17 Activity Duration Estimates: Safety Management
Systems   172

2.18 Duration Estimating Worksheet: Safety Management
Systems   174

2.19 Project Schedule: Safety Management Systems   176

2.20 Cost Management Plan: Safety Management Systems
                                                        178

2.21 Activity Cost Estimates: Safety Management Systems
                                                        180

2.22 Cost Estimating Worksheet: Safety Management
Systems   182

2.23 Cost Baseline: Safety Management Systems   184

2.24 Quality Management Plan: Safety Management
Systems   186

2.25 Quality Metrics: Safety Management Systems   188

2.26 Process Improvement Plan: Safety Management
Systems   190

2.27 Responsibility Assignment Matrix: Safety Management Systems   192

2.28 Roles and Responsibilities: Safety Management Systems   194

2.29 Human Resource Management Plan: Safety Management Systems   196

2.30 Communications Management Plan: Safety Management Systems   198

2.31 Risk Management Plan: Safety Management Systems   200

2.32 Risk Register: Safety Management Systems   202

2.33 Probability and Impact Assessment: Safety Management Systems   204

2.34 Probability and Impact Matrix: Safety Management Systems   206

2.35 Risk Data Sheet: Safety Management Systems   208

2.36 Procurement Management Plan: Safety Management Systems   210

2.37 Source Selection Criteria: Safety Management Systems   212

2.38 Stakeholder Management Plan: Safety Management Systems   214

2.39 Change Management Plan: Safety Management Systems   216

3.0 Executing Process Group: Safety Management Systems
218

3.1 Team Member Status Report: Safety Management
Systems   220

3.2 Change Request: Safety Management Systems   222

3.3 Change Log: Safety Management Systems   224

3.4 Decision Log: Safety Management Systems   226

3.5 Quality Audit: Safety Management Systems   228

3.6 Team Directory: Safety Management Systems   231

3.7 Team Operating Agreement: Safety Management
Systems   233

3.8 Team Performance Assessment: Safety Management
Systems   235

3.9 Team Member Performance Assessment: Safety
Management Systems   237

3.10 Issue Log: Safety Management Systems   239

4.0 Monitoring and Controlling Process Group: Safety
Management Systems   241

4.1 Project Performance Report: Safety Management
Systems   243

4.2 Variance Analysis: Safety Management Systems 245

4.3 Earned Value Status: Safety Management Systems 247

4.4 Risk Audit: Safety Management Systems   249

4.5 Contractor Status Report: Safety Management Systems
251

4.6 Formal Acceptance: Safety Management Systems   253

5.0 Closing Process Group: Safety Management Systems 255

5.1 Procurement Audit: Safety Management Systems   257

5.2 Contract Close-Out: Safety Management Systems   260

5.3 Project or Phase Close-Out: Safety Management Systems
262

5.4 Lessons Learned: Safety Management Systems   264
Index   266

About The Art of Service

The Art of Service, Business Process Architects since 2000, is dedicated to helping stakeholders achieve excellence.

Defining, designing, creating, and implementing a process to solve a stakeholders challenge or meet an objective is the most valuable role... In EVERY group, company, organization and department.

Unless you're talking a one-time, single-use project, there should be a process. Whether that process is managed and implemented by humans, AI, or a combination of the two, it needs to be designed by someone with a complex enough perspective to ask the right questions.

Someone capable of asking the right questions and step back and say, 'What are we really trying to accomplish here? And is there a different way to look at it?'

With The Art of Service's Standard Requirements Self-Assessments, we empower people who can do just that — whether their title is marketer, entrepreneur, manager, salesperson, consultant, Business Process Manager, executive assistant, IT Manager, CIO etc... —they are the people who rule the future. They are people who watch the process as it happens, and ask the right questions to make the process work better.

Contact us when you need any support with this Self-Assessment and any help with templates, blue-prints and examples of standard documents you might need:

http://theartofservice.com
service@theartofservice.com

Included Resources - how to access

Included with your purchase of the book is the Safety

Management Systems Self-Assessment Spreadsheet Dashboard which contains all questions and Self-Assessment areas and auto-generates insights, graphs, and project RACI planning - all with examples to get you started right away.

How? Simply send an email to
access@theartofservice.com
with this books' title in the subject to get the Safety Management Systems Self Assessment Tool right away.

You will receive the following contents with New and Updated specific criteria:

- The latest quick edition of the book in PDF

- The latest complete edition of the book in PDF, which criteria correspond to the criteria in...

- The Self-Assessment Excel Dashboard, and...

- Example pre-filled Self-Assessment Excel Dashboard to get familiar with results generation

- In-depth specific Checklists covering the topic

- Project management checklists and templates to assist with implementation

INCLUDES LIFETIME SELF ASSESSMENT UPDATES

Every self assessment comes with Lifetime Updates and Lifetime Free Updated Books. Lifetime Updates is an industry-first feature which allows you to receive verified self assessment updates, ensuring you always have the most accurate information at your fingertips.

Get it now- you will be glad you did - do it now, before you forget.

Send an email to **access@theartofservice.com** with this books' title in the subject to get the Safety Management Systems Self Assessment Tool right away.

Purpose of this Self-Assessment

This Self-Assessment has been developed to improve understanding of the requirements and elements of Safety Management Systems, based on best practices and standards in business process architecture, design and quality management.

It is designed to allow for a rapid Self-Assessment to determine how closely existing management practices and procedures correspond to the elements of the Self-Assessment.

The criteria of requirements and elements of Safety Management Systems have been rephrased in the format of a Self-Assessment questionnaire, with a seven-criterion scoring system, as explained in this document.

In this format, even with limited background knowledge of Safety Management Systems, a manager can quickly review existing operations to determine how they measure up to the standards. This in turn can serve as the starting point of a 'gap analysis' to identify management tools or system elements that might usefully be implemented in the organization to help improve overall performance.

How to use the Self-Assessment

On the following pages are a series of questions to identify to what extent your Safety Management Systems initiative is complete in comparison to the requirements set in standards.

To facilitate answering the questions, there is a space in front of each question to enter a score on a scale of '1' to '5'.

1 Strongly Disagree

2 Disagree

3 Neutral

4 Agree

5 Strongly Agree

Read the question and rate it with the following in front of mind:

'In my belief,
the answer to this question is clearly defined'.

There are two ways in which you can choose to interpret this statement;
1. how aware are you that the answer to the question is clearly defined
2. for more in-depth analysis you can choose to gather evidence and confirm the answer to the question. This obviously will take more time, most Self-Assessment users opt for the first way to interpret the question and dig deeper later on based on the outcome of the overall Self-Assessment.

A score of '1' would mean that the answer is not clear at all, where a '5' would mean the answer is crystal clear and defined. Leave emtpy when the question is not applicable or you don't want to answer it, you can skip it without affecting your score. Write your score in the space provided.

After you have responded to all the appropriate statements in each section, compute your average score for that section, using the formula provided, and round to the nearest tenth. Then transfer to the corresponding spoke in the Safety Management Systems Scorecard on the second next page of the Self-Assessment.

Your completed Safety Management Systems Scorecard will give you a clear presentation of which Safety Management Systems areas need attention.

Safety Management Systems Scorecard Example

Example of how the finalized Scorecard can look like:

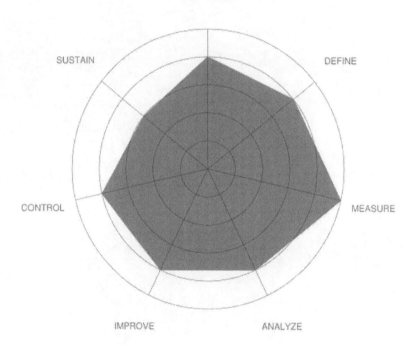

Safety Management Systems Scorecard

Your Scores:

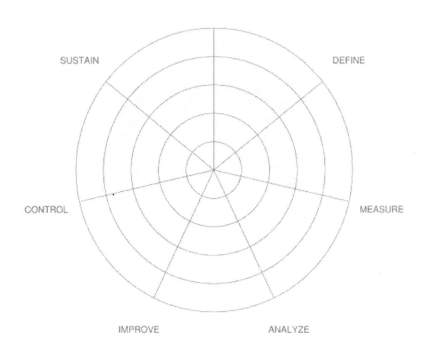

BEGINNING OF THE SELF-ASSESSMENT:

CRITERION #1: RECOGNIZE

INTENT: Be aware of the need for change. Recognize that there is an unfavorable variation, problem or symptom.

In my belief, the answer to this question is clearly defined:

5 Strongly Agree

4 Agree

3 Neutral

2 Disagree

1 Strongly Disagree

1. What Safety management systems events should you attend?
<--- Score

2. Who needs to know about Safety management systems?
<--- Score

3. Do you recognize Safety management systems

achievements?
<--- Score

4. How do you take a forward-looking perspective in identifying Safety management systems research related to market response and models?
<--- Score

5. Is it needed?
<--- Score

6. Are employees recognized or rewarded for performance that demonstrates the highest levels of integrity?
<--- Score

7. Does the problem have ethical dimensions?
<--- Score

8. Are your goals realistic? Do you need to redefine your problem? Perhaps the problem has changed or maybe you have reached your goal and need to set a new one?
<--- Score

9. Will new equipment/products be required to facilitate Safety management systems delivery, for example is new software needed?
<--- Score

10. How do you recognize an Safety management systems objection?
<--- Score

11. What needs to stay?
<--- Score

12. What are the stakeholder objectives to be achieved with Safety management systems?
<--- Score

13. Are there Safety management systems problems defined?
<--- Score

14. Think about the people you identified for your Safety management systems project and the project responsibilities you would assign to them, what kind of training do you think they would need to perform these responsibilities effectively?
<--- Score

15. What tools and technologies are needed for a custom Safety management systems project?
<--- Score

16. Will it solve real problems?
<--- Score

17. How are you going to measure success?
<--- Score

18. What are the clients issues and concerns?
<--- Score

19. How can auditing be a preventative security measure?
<--- Score

20. Does your organization need more Safety management systems education?
<--- Score

21. How are the Safety management systems's objectives aligned to the group's overall stakeholder strategy?
<--- Score

22. Who should resolve the Safety management systems issues?
<--- Score

23. What is the Safety management systems problem definition? What do you need to resolve?
<--- Score

24. What extra resources will you need?
<--- Score

25. Are there any specific expectations or concerns about the Safety management systems team, Safety management systems itself?
<--- Score

26. What do employees need in the short term?
<--- Score

27. How does it fit into your organizational needs and tasks?
<--- Score

28. Who defines the rules in relation to any given issue?
<--- Score

29. Consider your own Safety management systems project, what types of organizational problems do you think might be causing or affecting your problem,

based on the work done so far?
<--- Score

30. What is the problem and/or vulnerability?
<--- Score

31. Looking at each person individually – does every one have the qualities which are needed to work in this group?
<--- Score

32. Is it clear when you think of the day ahead of you what activities and tasks you need to complete?
<--- Score

33. Would you recognize a threat from the inside?
<--- Score

34. Where do you need to exercise leadership?
<--- Score

35. When a Safety management systems manager recognizes a problem, what options are available?
<--- Score

36. Are employees recognized for desired behaviors?
<--- Score

37. Who needs budgets?
<--- Score

38. What needs to be done?
<--- Score

39. What is the problem or issue?
<--- Score

40. What training and capacity building actions are needed to implement proposed reforms?
<--- Score

41. Where is training needed?
<--- Score

42. What prevents you from making the changes you know will make you a more effective Safety management systems leader?
<--- Score

43. Whom do you really need or want to serve?
<--- Score

44. Can management personnel recognize the monetary benefit of Safety management systems?
<--- Score

45. What are the minority interests and what amount of minority interests can be recognized?
<--- Score

46. What Safety management systems problem should be solved?
<--- Score

47. What are the timeframes required to resolve each of the issues/problems?
<--- Score

48. What is the extent or complexity of the Safety management systems problem?
<--- Score

49. What would happen if Safety management systems weren't done?
<--- Score

50. Why is this needed?
<--- Score

51. To what extent would your organization benefit from being recognized as a award recipient?
<--- Score

52. What information do users need?
<--- Score

53. What resources or support might you need?
<--- Score

54. What does Safety management systems success mean to the stakeholders?
<--- Score

55. What is the recognized need?
<--- Score

56. What do you need to start doing?
<--- Score

57. What situation(s) led to this Safety management systems Self Assessment?
<--- Score

58. What else needs to be measured?
<--- Score

59. Who needs to know?
<--- Score

60. Do you need to avoid or amend any Safety management systems activities?
<--- Score

61. As a sponsor, customer or management, how important is it to meet goals, objectives?
<--- Score

62. How do you identify the kinds of information that you will need?
<--- Score

63. Is the quality assurance team identified?
<--- Score

64. Why the need?
<--- Score

65. Do you know what you need to know about Safety management systems?
<--- Score

66. What problems are you facing and how do you consider Safety management systems will circumvent those obstacles?
<--- Score

67. What should be considered when identifying available resources, constraints, and deadlines?
<--- Score

68. Do you have/need 24-hour access to key personnel?
<--- Score

69. Are losses recognized in a timely manner?
<--- Score

70. For your Safety management systems project, identify and describe the business environment, is there more than one layer to the business environment?
<--- Score

71. Does Safety management systems create potential expectations in other areas that need to be recognized and considered?
<--- Score

72. What is the smallest subset of the problem you can usefully solve?
<--- Score

73. What are your needs in relation to Safety management systems skills, labor, equipment, and markets?
<--- Score

74. Who are your key stakeholders who need to sign off?
<--- Score

75. Who else hopes to benefit from it?
<--- Score

76. What are the expected benefits of Safety management systems to the stakeholder?
<--- Score

77. What activities does the governance board need to consider?

<--- Score

78. Are controls defined to recognize and contain problems?
<--- Score

79. What creative shifts do you need to take?
<--- Score

80. Did you miss any major Safety management systems issues?
<--- Score

81. Which information does the Safety management systems business case need to include?
<--- Score

82. How do you assess your Safety management systems workforce capability and capacity needs, including skills, competencies, and staffing levels?
<--- Score

83. What vendors make products that address the Safety management systems needs?
<--- Score

84. Will Safety management systems deliverables need to be tested and, if so, by whom?
<--- Score

85. How much are sponsors, customers, partners, stakeholders involved in Safety management systems? In other words, what are the risks, if Safety management systems does not deliver successfully?
<--- Score

86. Are there regulatory / compliance issues?
<--- Score

87. What Safety management systems capabilities do you need?
<--- Score

88. Are there recognized Safety management systems problems?
<--- Score

89. Have you identified your Safety management systems key performance indicators?
<--- Score

90. How are training requirements identified?
<--- Score

91. Who needs what information?
<--- Score

92. To what extent does each concerned units management team recognize Safety management systems as an effective investment?
<--- Score

93. Are there any revenue recognition issues?
<--- Score

94. What Safety management systems coordination do you need?
<--- Score

95. Do you need different information or graphics?
<--- Score

96. How many trainings, in total, are needed?
<--- Score

97. Are problem definition and motivation clearly presented?
<--- Score

98. Which issues are too important to ignore?
<--- Score

Add up total points for this section:
_____ = Total points for this section

Divided by: _____ (number of statements answered) = _____
Average score for this section

Transfer your score to the Safety management systems Index at the beginning of the Self-Assessment.

CRITERION #2: DEFINE:

INTENT: Formulate the stakeholder problem. Define the problem, needs and objectives.

In my belief, the answer to this question is clearly defined:

5 Strongly Agree

4 Agree

3 Neutral

2 Disagree

1 Strongly Disagree

1. What is the scope?
<--- Score

2. Is the scope of Safety management systems defined?
<--- Score

3. Are resources adequate for the scope?
<--- Score

4. Is special Safety management systems user knowledge required?
<--- Score

5. Are there different segments of customers?
<--- Score

6. Is there a critical path to deliver Safety management systems results?
<--- Score

7. Is there regularly 100% attendance at the team meetings? If not, have appointed substitutes attended to preserve cross-functionality and full representation?
<--- Score

8. How do you gather requirements?
<--- Score

9. How can the value of Safety management systems be defined?
<--- Score

10. Are different versions of process maps needed to account for the different types of inputs?
<--- Score

11. What are the compelling stakeholder reasons for embarking on Safety management systems?
<--- Score

12. How and when will the baselines be defined?
<--- Score

13. Is the Safety management systems scope complete and appropriately sized?
<--- Score

14. What are the record-keeping requirements of Safety management systems activities?
<--- Score

15. What happens if Safety management systems's scope changes?
<--- Score

16. How did the Safety management systems manager receive input to the development of a Safety management systems improvement plan and the estimated completion dates/times of each activity?
<--- Score

17. What sort of initial information to gather?
<--- Score

18. What information should you gather?
<--- Score

19. Will team members regularly document their Safety management systems work?
<--- Score

20. Has your scope been defined?
<--- Score

21. Do you have organizational privacy requirements?
<--- Score

22. What baselines are required to be defined and managed?

<--- Score

23. Has anyone else (internal or external to the group) attempted to solve this problem or a similar one before? If so, what knowledge can be leveraged from these previous efforts?
<--- Score

24. What constraints exist that might impact the team?
<--- Score

25. When are meeting minutes sent out? Who is on the distribution list?
<--- Score

26. Do you have a Safety management systems success story or case study ready to tell and share?
<--- Score

27. Scope of sensitive information?
<--- Score

28. How would you define Safety management systems leadership?
<--- Score

29. What is a worst-case scenario for losses?
<--- Score

30. Who are the Safety management systems improvement team members, including Management Leads and Coaches?
<--- Score

31. Do you all define Safety management systems in

the same way?
<--- Score

32. What defines best in class?
<--- Score

33. How does the Safety management systems manager ensure against scope creep?
<--- Score

34. How do you catch Safety management systems definition inconsistencies?
<--- Score

35. What Safety management systems requirements should be gathered?
<--- Score

36. What customer feedback methods were used to solicit their input?
<--- Score

37. Is the team adequately staffed with the desired cross-functionality? If not, what additional resources are available to the team?
<--- Score

38. Will team members perform Safety management systems work when assigned and in a timely fashion?
<--- Score

39. Do the problem and goal statements meet the SMART criteria (specific, measurable, attainable, relevant, and time-bound)?
<--- Score

40. What are the boundaries of the scope? What is in bounds and what is not? What is the start point? What is the stop point?
<--- Score

41. Will a Safety management systems production readiness review be required?
<--- Score

42. Have all of the relationships been defined properly?
<--- Score

43. What intelligence can you gather?
<--- Score

44. Are roles and responsibilities formally defined?
<--- Score

45. How is the team tracking and documenting its work?
<--- Score

46. How do you gather the stories?
<--- Score

47. How do you gather Safety management systems requirements?
<--- Score

48. What is out of scope?
<--- Score

49. What is the definition of success?
<--- Score

50. Is Safety management systems required?
<--- Score

51. What is the definition of Safety management systems excellence?
<--- Score

52. Is the improvement team aware of the different versions of a process: what they think it is vs. what it actually is vs. what it should be vs. what it could be?
<--- Score

53. What are the tasks and definitions?
<--- Score.

54. Is there a clear Safety management systems case definition?
<--- Score

55. Has the Safety management systems work been fairly and/or equitably divided and delegated among team members who are qualified and capable to perform the work? Has everyone contributed?
<--- Score

56. What are the dynamics of the communication plan?
<--- Score

57. What system do you use for gathering Safety management systems information?
<--- Score

58. When is the estimated completion date?
<--- Score

59. Has a Safety management systems requirement not been met?
<--- Score

60. How would you define the culture at your organization, how susceptible is it to Safety management systems changes?
<--- Score

61. Is the work to date meeting requirements?
<--- Score

62. Is data collected and displayed to better understand customer(s) critical needs and requirements.
<--- Score

63. What are the Roles and Responsibilities for each team member and its leadership? Where is this documented?
<--- Score

64. Does the scope remain the same?
<--- Score

65. Who is gathering information?
<--- Score

66. Is Safety management systems currently on schedule according to the plan?
<--- Score

67. What information do you gather?
<--- Score

68. Are the Safety management systems requirements

testable?
<--- Score

69. What are the core elements of the Safety management systems business case?
<--- Score

70. What is in scope?
<--- Score

71. Are all requirements met?
<--- Score

72. What scope to assess?
<--- Score

73. Are the Safety management systems requirements complete?
<--- Score

74. Has a team charter been developed and communicated?
<--- Score

75. In what way can you redefine the criteria of choice clients have in your category in your favor?
<--- Score

76. Has/have the customer(s) been identified?
<--- Score

77. What are the Safety management systems tasks and definitions?
<--- Score

78. Are audit criteria, scope, frequency and methods

defined?
<--- Score

79. Are there any constraints known that bear on the ability to perform Safety management systems work? How is the team addressing them?
<--- Score

80. How was the 'as is' process map developed, reviewed, verified and validated?
<--- Score

81. What scope do you want your strategy to cover?
<--- Score

82. Is there a Safety management systems management charter, including stakeholder case, problem and goal statements, scope, milestones, roles and responsibilities, communication plan?
<--- Score

83. How do you think the partners involved in Safety management systems would have defined success?
<--- Score

84. How have you defined all Safety management systems requirements first?
<--- Score

85. Are accountability and ownership for Safety management systems clearly defined?
<--- Score

86. Has a high-level 'as is' process map been completed, verified and validated?
<--- Score

87. How are consistent Safety management systems definitions important?
<--- Score

88. How will the Safety management systems team and the group measure complete success of Safety management systems?
<--- Score

89. Is there a completed, verified, and validated high-level 'as is' (not 'should be' or 'could be') stakeholder process map?
<--- Score

90. What are the rough order estimates on cost savings/opportunities that Safety management systems brings?
<--- Score

91. How do you manage scope?
<--- Score

92. What knowledge or experience is required?
<--- Score

93. Is the team equipped with available and reliable resources?
<--- Score

94. What sources do you use to gather information for a Safety management systems study?
<--- Score

95. Is the current 'as is' process being followed? If not, what are the discrepancies?

<--- Score

96. Are approval levels defined for contracts and supplements to contracts?
<--- Score

97. Have all basic functions of Safety management systems been defined?
<--- Score

98. What is in the scope and what is not in scope?
<--- Score

99. Why are you doing Safety management systems and what is the scope?
<--- Score

100. What are (control) requirements for Safety management systems Information?
<--- Score

101. How will variation in the actual durations of each activity be dealt with to ensure that the expected Safety management systems results are met?
<--- Score

102. If substitutes have been appointed, have they been briefed on the Safety management systems goals and received regular communications as to the progress to date?
<--- Score

103. How do you keep key subject matter experts in the loop?
<--- Score

104. What specifically is the problem? Where does it occur? When does it occur? What is its extent?
<--- Score

105. What are the Safety management systems use cases?
<--- Score

106. When is/was the Safety management systems start date?
<--- Score

107. How do you manage changes in Safety management systems requirements?
<--- Score

108. What is out-of-scope initially?
<--- Score

109. Has everyone on the team, including the team leaders, been properly trained?
<--- Score

110. Are customer(s) identified and segmented according to their different needs and requirements?
<--- Score

111. Is it clearly defined in and to your organization what you do?
<--- Score

112. What is the worst case scenario?
<--- Score

113. Does the team have regular meetings?
<--- Score

114. Is Safety management systems linked to key stakeholder goals and objectives?
<--- Score

115. Has the improvement team collected the 'voice of the customer' (obtained feedback – qualitative and quantitative)?
<--- Score

116. Who defines (or who defined) the rules and roles?
<--- Score

117. How do you hand over Safety management systems context?
<--- Score

118. What would be the goal or target for a Safety management systems's improvement team?
<--- Score

119. Is there a completed SIPOC representation, describing the Suppliers, Inputs, Process, Outputs, and Customers?
<--- Score

120. What gets examined?
<--- Score

121. What is the scope of the Safety management systems work?
<--- Score

122. What is the scope of Safety management systems?
<--- Score

123. Is the Safety management systems scope manageable?
<--- Score

124. What key stakeholder process output measure(s) does Safety management systems leverage and how?
<--- Score

125. Is scope creep really all bad news?
<--- Score

126. Has the direction changed at all during the course of Safety management systems? If so, when did it change and why?
<--- Score

127. Are required metrics defined, what are they?
<--- Score

128. Are task requirements clearly defined?
<--- Score

129. What critical content must be communicated – who, what, when, where, and how?
<--- Score

130. Have the customer needs been translated into specific, measurable requirements? How?
<--- Score

131. What is the context?
<--- Score

132. Who approved the Safety management systems scope?

<--- Score

133. How often are the team meetings?
<--- Score

134. Who is gathering Safety management systems information?
<--- Score

135. What was the context?
<--- Score

136. What are the requirements for audit information?
<--- Score

137. Has a project plan, Gantt chart, or similar been developed/completed?
<--- Score

Add up total points for this section:
_ _ _ _ _ = Total points for this section

Divided by: _ _ _ _ _ _ (number of statements answered) = _ _ _ _ _ _
Average score for this section

Transfer your score to the Safety management systems Index at the beginning of the Self-Assessment.

CRITERION #3: MEASURE:

INTENT: Gather the correct data.
Measure the current performance and
evolution of the situation.

In my belief, the answer to this
question is clearly defined:

5 Strongly Agree

4 Agree

3 Neutral

2 Disagree

1 Strongly Disagree

1. When are costs are incurred?
<--- Score

2. What are the costs of reform?
<--- Score

3. What disadvantage does this cause for the user?
<--- Score

4. What is your Safety management systems quality cost segregation study?
<--- Score

5. How will measures be used to manage and adapt?
<--- Score

6. Is the cost worth the Safety management systems effort ?
<--- Score

7. Do you aggressively reward and promote the people who have the biggest impact on creating excellent Safety management systems services/ products?
<--- Score

8. Do the benefits outweigh the costs?
<--- Score

9. How do you verify performance?
<--- Score

10. How can you reduce the costs of obtaining inputs?
<--- Score

11. Are you aware of what could cause a problem?
<--- Score

12. What evidence is there and what is measured?
<--- Score

13. What is your decision requirements diagram?
<--- Score

14. How do you aggregate measures across priorities?

<--- Score

15. Are indirect costs charged to the Safety management systems program?
<--- Score

16. Are the measurements objective?
<--- Score

17. Who should receive measurement reports?
<--- Score

18. Are the units of measure consistent?
<--- Score

19. Is the solution cost-effective?
<--- Score

20. Did you tackle the cause or the symptom?
<--- Score

21. Are there any easy-to-implement alternatives to Safety management systems? Sometimes other solutions are available that do not require the cost implications of a full-blown project?
<--- Score

22. What are hidden Safety management systems quality costs?
<--- Score

23. How will you measure success?
<--- Score

24. How do you prevent mis-estimating cost?
<--- Score

25. Are the Safety management systems benefits worth its costs?
<--- Score

26. Does a Safety management systems quantification method exist?
<--- Score

27. Do you have a flow diagram of what happens?
<--- Score

28. What are the estimated costs of proposed changes?
<--- Score

29. Are supply costs steady or fluctuating?
<--- Score

30. What causes innovation to fail or succeed in your organization?
<--- Score

31. Was a business case (cost/benefit) developed?
<--- Score

32. How do you measure efficient delivery of Safety management systems services?
<--- Score

33. At what cost?
<--- Score

34. How are measurements made?
<--- Score

35. What do you measure and why?
<--- Score

36. How will you measure your Safety management systems effectiveness?
<--- Score

37. What is the total fixed cost?
<--- Score

38. What are your customers expectations and measures?
<--- Score

39. Does the Safety management systems task fit the client's priorities?
<--- Score

40. How do you measure success?
<--- Score

41. Which Safety management systems impacts are significant?
<--- Score

42. What are the uncertainties surrounding estimates of impact?
<--- Score

43. What would it cost to replace your technology?
<--- Score

44. How frequently do you track Safety management systems measures?
<--- Score

45. How will success or failure be measured?
<--- Score

46. When should you bother with diagrams?
<--- Score

47. What tests verify requirements?
<--- Score

48. How much does it cost?
<--- Score

49. What are the Safety management systems investment costs?
<--- Score

50. How will effects be measured?
<--- Score

51. What drives O&M cost?
<--- Score

52. How do you verify if Safety management systems is built right?
<--- Score

53. What are the Safety management systems key cost drivers?
<--- Score

54. How can you measure Safety management systems in a systematic way?
<--- Score

55. What would be a real cause for concern?
<--- Score

56. Why do you expend time and effort to implement measurement, for whom?
<--- Score

57. Among the Safety management systems product and service cost to be estimated, which is considered hardest to estimate?
<--- Score

58. What are the costs of delaying Safety management systems action?
<--- Score

59. What causes mismanagement?
<--- Score

60. Have design-to-cost goals been established?
<--- Score

61. Is it possible to estimate the impact of unanticipated complexity such as wrong or failed assumptions, feedback, etcetera on proposed reforms?
<--- Score

62. How do you verify your resources?
<--- Score

63. When a disaster occurs, who gets priority?
<--- Score

64. What are the strategic priorities for this year?
<--- Score

65. Where is it measured?

<--- Score

66. How will your organization measure success?
<--- Score

67. Are there competing Safety management systems priorities?
<--- Score

68. Are Safety management systems vulnerabilities categorized and prioritized?
<--- Score

69. What is measured? Why?
<--- Score

70. Are you taking your company in the direction of better and revenue or cheaper and cost?
<--- Score

71. How will costs be allocated?
<--- Score

72. What is the total cost related to deploying Safety management systems, including any consulting or professional services?
<--- Score

73. What do people want to verify?
<--- Score

74. What are the costs?
<--- Score

75. What are the types and number of measures to use?

<--- Score

76. How is progress measured?
<--- Score

77. What could cause delays in the schedule?
<--- Score

78. What is the Safety management systems business impact?
<--- Score

79. How do you verify the Safety management systems requirements quality?
<--- Score

80. How do your measurements capture actionable Safety management systems information for use in exceeding your customers expectations and securing your customers engagement?
<--- Score

81. What could cause you to change course?
<--- Score

82. What can be used to verify compliance?
<--- Score

83. Have you included everything in your Safety management systems cost models?
<--- Score

84. How can you measure the performance?
<--- Score

85. Is there an opportunity to verify requirements?

<--- Score

86. What relevant entities could be measured?
<--- Score

87. What are your operating costs?
<--- Score

88. Are missed Safety management systems opportunities costing your organization money?
<--- Score

89. How can you reduce costs?
<--- Score

90. Who pays the cost?
<--- Score

91. How do you quantify and qualify impacts?
<--- Score

92. What users will be impacted?
<--- Score

93. How is performance measured?
<--- Score

94. How long to keep data and how to manage retention costs?
<--- Score

95. How to cause the change?
<--- Score

96. What does a Test Case verify?
<--- Score

97. How do you verify and validate the Safety management systems data?
<--- Score

98. What does losing customers cost your organization?
<--- Score

99. What causes investor action?
<--- Score

100. Do you have an issue in getting priority?
<--- Score

101. Are actual costs in line with budgeted costs?
<--- Score

102. What causes extra work or rework?
<--- Score

103. What is the root cause(s) of the problem?
<--- Score

104. What methods are feasible and acceptable to estimate the impact of reforms?
<--- Score

105. Do you have any cost Safety management systems limitation requirements?
<--- Score

106. Have you made assumptions about the shape of the future, particularly its impact on your customers and competitors?
<--- Score

107. What happens if cost savings do not materialize?
<--- Score

108. What does your operating model cost?
<--- Score

109. Are there measurements based on task performance?
<--- Score

110. How do you measure lifecycle phases?
<--- Score

111. How do you measure variability?
<--- Score

112. Has a cost center been established?
<--- Score

113. Does management have the right priorities among projects?
<--- Score

114. How do you control the overall costs of your work processes?
<--- Score

115. Which measures and indicators matter?
<--- Score

116. Which costs should be taken into account?
<--- Score

117. How can you manage cost down?
<--- Score

118. Why do the measurements/indicators matter?
<--- Score

119. How do you verify the authenticity of the data and information used?
<--- Score

120. What potential environmental factors impact the Safety management systems effort?
<--- Score

121. What are your key Safety management systems organizational performance measures, including key short and longer-term financial measures?
<--- Score

122. What are the costs and benefits?
<--- Score

123. What measurements are being captured?
<--- Score

124. What harm might be caused?
<--- Score

125. How is the value delivered by Safety management systems being measured?
<--- Score

126. How sensitive must the Safety management systems strategy be to cost?
<--- Score

127. What is the cause of any Safety management systems gaps?

<--- Score

128. How are costs allocated?
<--- Score

129. What is an unallowable cost?
<--- Score

130. What is the cost of rework?
<--- Score

131. Where is the cost?
<--- Score

Add up total points for this section:
_____ = Total points for this section

Divided by: _____ (number of
statements answered) = _____
Average score for this section

Transfer your score to the Safety
management systems Index at the
beginning of the Self-Assessment.

CRITERION #4: ANALYZE:

INTENT: Analyze causes, assumptions and hypotheses.

In my belief, the answer to this question is clearly defined:

5 Strongly Agree

4 Agree

3 Neutral

2 Disagree

1 Strongly Disagree

1. What tools were used to narrow the list of possible causes?
<--- Score

2. How much data can be collected in the given timeframe?
<--- Score

3. Were any designed experiments used to generate additional insight into the data analysis?

<--- Score

4. Record-keeping requirements flow from the records needed as inputs, outputs, controls and for transformation of a Safety management systems process, are the records needed as inputs to the Safety management systems process available?
<--- Score

5. What were the crucial 'moments of truth' on the process map?
<--- Score

6. What tools were used to generate the list of possible causes?
<--- Score

7. What are the necessary qualifications?
<--- Score

8. Has an output goal been set?
<--- Score

9. How difficult is it to qualify what Safety management systems ROI is?
<--- Score

10. How do you identify specific Safety management systems investment opportunities and emerging trends?
<--- Score

11. Are gaps between current performance and the goal performance identified?
<--- Score

12. How is data used for program management and improvement?
<--- Score

13. What qualifications are needed?
<--- Score

14. Is the performance gap determined?
<--- Score

15. What process should you select for improvement?
<--- Score

16. Where can you get qualified talent today?
<--- Score

17. Were there any improvement opportunities identified from the process analysis?
<--- Score

18. Who will gather what data?
<--- Score

19. What is the oversight process?
<--- Score

20. When should a process be art not science?
<--- Score

21. How do you promote understanding that opportunity for improvement is not criticism of the status quo, or the people who created the status quo?
<--- Score

22. Do quality systems drive continuous improvement?

<--- Score

23. Is the final output clearly identified?
<--- Score

24. What qualifies as competition?
<--- Score

25. What are your current levels and trends in key Safety management systems measures or indicators of product and process performance that are important to and directly serve your customers?
<--- Score

26. What are the best opportunities for value improvement?
<--- Score

27. How many input/output points does it require?
<--- Score

28. What data do you need to collect?
<--- Score

29. What, related to, Safety management systems processes does your organization outsource?
<--- Score

30. What other organizational variables, such as reward systems or communication systems, affect the performance of this Safety management systems process?
<--- Score

31. What Safety management systems data will be collected?

<--- Score

32. What resources go in to get the desired output?
<--- Score

33. What other jobs or tasks affect the performance of the steps in the Safety management systems process?
<--- Score

34. Has data output been validated?
<--- Score

35. How do you use Safety management systems data and information to support organizational decision making and innovation?
<--- Score

36. Who gets your output?
<--- Score

37. What information qualified as important?
<--- Score

38. Who is involved with workflow mapping?
<--- Score

39. What are your current levels and trends in key measures or indicators of Safety management systems product and process performance that are important to and directly serve your customers? How do these results compare with the performance of your competitors and other organizations with similar offerings?
<--- Score

40. Did any additional data need to be collected?

<--- Score

41. What Safety management systems metrics are outputs of the process?
<--- Score

42. Is the gap/opportunity displayed and communicated in financial terms?
<--- Score

43. What are the Safety management systems design outputs?
<--- Score

44. What did the team gain from developing a sub-process map?
<--- Score

45. Are you missing Safety management systems opportunities?
<--- Score

46. What quality tools were used to get through the analyze phase?
<--- Score

47. What is the output?
<--- Score

48. How are outputs preserved and protected?
<--- Score

49. Where is Safety management systems data gathered?
<--- Score

50. Can you add value to the current Safety management systems decision-making process (largely qualitative) by incorporating uncertainty modeling (more quantitative)?
<--- Score

51. Who is involved in the management review process?
<--- Score

52. How do you measure the operational performance of your key work systems and processes, including productivity, cycle time, and other appropriate measures of process effectiveness, efficiency, and innovation?
<--- Score

53. Identify an operational issue in your organization, for example, could a particular task be done more quickly or more efficiently by Safety management systems?
<--- Score

54. What are the revised rough estimates of the financial savings/opportunity for Safety management systems improvements?
<--- Score

55. What is the cost of poor quality as supported by the team's analysis?
<--- Score

56. Should you invest in industry-recognized qualifications?
<--- Score

57. What qualifications do Safety management systems leaders need?
<--- Score

58. What do you need to qualify?
<--- Score

59. What process improvements will be needed?
<--- Score

60. Do you have the authority to produce the output?
<--- Score

61. What is your organizations process which leads to recognition of value generation?
<--- Score

62. How will corresponding data be collected?
<--- Score

63. Are Safety management systems changes recognized early enough to be approved through the regular process?
<--- Score

64. What successful thing are you doing today that may be blinding you to new growth opportunities?
<--- Score

65. What Safety management systems data should be managed?
<--- Score

66. Who qualifies to gain access to data?
<--- Score

67. How can risk management be tied procedurally to process elements?
<--- Score

68. How do you ensure that the Safety management systems opportunity is realistic?
<--- Score

69. Who owns what data?
<--- Score

70. What are the Safety management systems business drivers?
<--- Score

71. Are all staff in core Safety management systems subjects Highly Qualified?
<--- Score

72. Was a cause-and-effect diagram used to explore the different types of causes (or sources of variation)?
<--- Score

73. What data is gathered?
<--- Score

74. Have the problem and goal statements been updated to reflect the additional knowledge gained from the analyze phase?
<--- Score

75. What kind of crime could a potential new hire have committed that would not only not disqualify him/her from being hired by your organization, but would actually indicate that he/she might be a particularly good fit?

<--- Score

76. How is Safety management systems data gathered?
<--- Score

77. Is data and process analysis, root cause analysis and quantifying the gap/opportunity in place?
<--- Score

78. Are all team members qualified for all tasks?
<--- Score

79. How will the change process be managed?
<--- Score

80. How do your work systems and key work processes relate to and capitalize on your core competencies?
<--- Score

81. How is the data gathered?
<--- Score

82. What Safety management systems data do you gather or use now?
<--- Score

83. How was the detailed process map generated, verified, and validated?
<--- Score

84. What is the complexity of the output produced?
<--- Score

85. How do mission and objectives affect the Safety

management systems processes of your organization?
<--- Score

86. Do you understand your management processes today?
<--- Score

87. What are the personnel training and qualifications required?
<--- Score

88. What Safety management systems data should be collected?
<--- Score

89. How will the Safety management systems data be captured?
<--- Score

90. What does the data say about the performance of the stakeholder process?
<--- Score

91. Who will facilitate the team and process?
<--- Score

92. How will the data be checked for quality?
<--- Score

93. Was a detailed process map created to amplify critical steps of the 'as is' stakeholder process?
<--- Score

94. What is the Value Stream Mapping?
<--- Score

95. How is the way you as the leader think and process information affecting your organizational culture?
<--- Score

96. If integrated quality and safety management systems could become business drivers and pathways for productivity growth, is the same true for integrated security management?
<--- Score

97. What conclusions were drawn from the team's data collection and analysis? How did the team reach these conclusions?
<--- Score

98. Which Safety management systems data should be retained?
<--- Score

99. Is there an established change management process?
<--- Score

100. What are your outputs?
<--- Score

101. How is the Safety management systems Value Stream Mapping managed?
<--- Score

102. Is pre-qualification of suppliers carried out?
<--- Score

103. What systems/processes must you excel at?
<--- Score

104. What internal processes need improvement?
<--- Score

105. What is your organizations system for selecting qualified vendors?
<--- Score

106. What were the financial benefits resulting from any 'ground fruit or low-hanging fruit' (quick fixes)?
<--- Score

107. Is the suppliers process defined and controlled?
<--- Score

108. Have any additional benefits been identified that will result from closing all or most of the gaps?
<--- Score

109. Is there a strict change management process?
<--- Score

110. Do your contracts/agreements contain data security obligations?
<--- Score

111. Do your employees have the opportunity to do what they do best everyday?
<--- Score

112. What is the Safety management systems Driver?
<--- Score

113. Did any value-added analysis or 'lean thinking' take place to identify some of the gaps shown on the 'as is' process map?
<--- Score

114. Have you defined which data is gathered how?
<--- Score

115. What are the processes for audit reporting and management?
<--- Score

116. What training and qualifications will you need?
<--- Score

117. An organizationally feasible system request is one that considers the mission, goals and objectives of the organization, key questions are: is the Safety management systems solution request practical and will it solve a problem or take advantage of an opportunity to achieve company goals?
<--- Score

118. A compounding model resolution with available relevant data can often provide insight towards a solution methodology; which Safety management systems models, tools and techniques are necessary?
<--- Score

119. How do you define collaboration and team output?
<--- Score

120. What methods do you use to gather Safety management systems data?
<--- Score

121. Is the Safety management systems process severely broken such that a re-design is necessary?
<--- Score

122. Do staff qualifications match your project?
<--- Score

123. Think about some of the processes you undertake within your organization, which do you own?
<--- Score

124. What controls do you have in place to protect data?
<--- Score

125. What qualifications are necessary?
<--- Score·

126. Do several people in different organizational units assist with the Safety management systems process?
<--- Score

127. How has the Safety management systems data been gathered?
<--- Score

128. Is there any way to speed up the process?
<--- Score

129. How does the organization define, manage, and improve its Safety management systems processes?
<--- Score

130. What are the disruptive Safety management systems technologies that enable your organization to radically change your business processes?
<--- Score

131. Were Pareto charts (or similar) used to portray the 'heavy hitters' (or key sources of variation)?
<--- Score

132. How often will data be collected for measures?
<--- Score

133. What are your key performance measures or indicators and in-process measures for the control and improvement of your Safety management systems processes?
<--- Score

134. What types of data do your Safety management systems indicators require?
<--- Score

135. What are your best practices for minimizing Safety management systems project risk, while demonstrating incremental value and quick wins throughout the Safety management systems project lifecycle?
<--- Score

Add up total points for this section:
_____ = Total points for this section

Divided by: _____ (number of statements answered) = _____
Average score for this section

Transfer your score to the Safety management systems Index at the beginning of the Self-Assessment.

CRITERION #5: IMPROVE:

INTENT: Develop a practical solution.
Innovate, establish and test the
solution and to measure the results.

In my belief, the answer to this
question is clearly defined:

5 Strongly Agree

4 Agree

3 Neutral

2 Disagree

1 Strongly Disagree

1. What are the implications of the one critical Safety
management systems decision 10 minutes, 10
months, and 10 years from now?
<--- Score

2. Would you develop a Safety management systems
Communication Strategy?
<--- Score

3. How will you measure the results?
<--- Score

4. What are the concrete Safety management systems results?
<--- Score

5. Are the risks fully understood, reasonable and manageable?
<--- Score

6. Have you identified breakpoints and/or risk tolerances that will trigger broad consideration of a potential need for intervention or modification of strategy?
<--- Score

7. Were any criteria developed to assist the team in testing and evaluating potential solutions?
<--- Score

8. Risk events: what are the things that could go wrong?
<--- Score

9. Safety management systems risk decisions: whose call Is It?
<--- Score

10. What is the risk?
<--- Score

11. Does a good decision guarantee a good outcome?
<--- Score

12. What do you want to improve?

<--- Score

13. Are decisions made in a timely manner?
<--- Score

14. How does the team improve its work?
<--- Score

15. How do you deal with Safety management systems risk?
<--- Score

16. What are the expected Safety management systems results?
<--- Score

17. Who will be responsible for making the decisions to include or exclude requested changes once Safety management systems is underway?
<--- Score

18. What is the team's contingency plan for potential problems occurring in implementation?
<--- Score

19. What area needs the greatest improvement?
<--- Score

20. What tools were used to evaluate the potential solutions?
<--- Score

21. How can you improve Safety management systems?
<--- Score

22. Are risk triggers captured?
<--- Score

23. Who manages Safety management systems risk?
<--- Score

24. How do you define the solutions' scope?
<--- Score

25. What error proofing will be done to address some of the discrepancies observed in the 'as is' process?
<--- Score

26. What lessons, if any, from a pilot were incorporated into the design of the full-scale solution?
<--- Score

27. How do you improve Safety management systems service perception, and satisfaction?
<--- Score

28. Is there any other Safety management systems solution?
<--- Score

29. Who manages supplier risk management in your organization?
<--- Score

30. How will you recognize and celebrate results?
<--- Score

31. Can you identify any significant risks or exposures to Safety management systems third- parties (vendors, service providers, alliance partners etc) that concern you?

<--- Score

32. What were the criteria for evaluating a Safety management systems pilot?
<--- Score

33. What improvements have been achieved?
<--- Score

34. Who controls key decisions that will be made?
<--- Score

35. How do you manage and improve your Safety management systems work systems to deliver customer value and achieve organizational success and sustainability?
<--- Score

36. Is the Safety management systems risk managed?
<--- Score

37. Do you need to do a usability evaluation?
<--- Score

38. How can you better manage risk?
<--- Score

39. Are procedures documented for managing Safety management systems risks?
<--- Score

40. How do you measure improved Safety management systems service perception, and satisfaction?
<--- Score

41. Who makes the Safety management systems decisions in your organization?
<--- Score

42. What attendant changes will need to be made to ensure that the solution is successful?
<--- Score

43. What resources are required for the improvement efforts?
<--- Score

44. Do you cover the five essential competencies: Communication, Collaboration,Innovation, Adaptability, and Leadership that improve an organizations ability to leverage the new Safety management systems in a volatile global economy?
<--- Score

45. What risks do you need to manage?
<--- Score

46. Is any Safety management systems documentation required?
<--- Score

47. Who do you report Safety management systems results to?
<--- Score

48. Is there a high likelihood that any recommendations will achieve their intended results?
<--- Score

49. How do you mitigate Safety management systems risk?

<--- Score

50. Which of the recognised risks out of all risks can be most likely transferred?
<--- Score

51. Are risk management tasks balanced centrally and locally?
<--- Score

52. In the past few months, what is the smallest change you have made that has had the biggest positive result? What was it about that small change that produced the large return?
<--- Score

53. What does the 'should be' process map/design look like?
<--- Score

54. Are events managed to resolution?
<--- Score

55. For decision problems, how do you develop a decision statement?
<--- Score

56. What criteria will you use to assess your Safety management systems risks?
<--- Score

57. Who will be responsible for documenting the Safety management systems requirements in detail?
<--- Score

58. How risky is your organization?

<--- Score

59. How will you know when its improved?
<--- Score

60. How will you know that you have improved?
<--- Score

61. When you map the key players in your own work and the types/domains of relationships with them, which relationships do you find easy and which challenging, and why?
<--- Score

62. What communications are necessary to support the implementation of the solution?
<--- Score

63. Does the goal represent a desired result that can be measured?
<--- Score

64. Who are the Safety management systems decision makers?
<--- Score

65. What should a proof of concept or pilot accomplish?
<--- Score

66. Who are the people involved in developing and implementing Safety management systems?
<--- Score

67. What went well, what should change, what can improve?

<--- Score

68. How do you link measurement and risk?
<--- Score

69. What tools were most useful during the improve phase?
<--- Score

70. For estimation problems, how do you develop an estimation statement?
<--- Score

71. Have you achieved Safety management systems improvements?
<--- Score

72. Are the key business and technology risks being managed?
<--- Score

73. Is the Safety management systems solution sustainable?
<--- Score

74. What were the underlying assumptions on the cost-benefit analysis?
<--- Score

75. Are the most efficient solutions problem-specific?
<--- Score

76. Who will be using the results of the measurement activities?
<--- Score

77. Do you have the optimal project management team structure?
<--- Score

78. How are policy decisions made and where?
<--- Score

79. What strategies for Safety management systems improvement are successful?
<--- Score

80. How is knowledge sharing about risk management improved?
<--- Score

81. How do you improve productivity?
<--- Score

82. Is the solution technically practical?
<--- Score

83. What practices helps your organization to develop its capacity to recognize patterns?
<--- Score

84. Which Safety management systems solution is appropriate?
<--- Score

85. Was a Safety management systems charter developed?
<--- Score

86. Explorations of the frontiers of Safety management systems will help you build influence, improve Safety management systems, optimize

decision making, and sustain change, what is your approach?
<--- Score

87. What are the affordable Safety management systems risks?
<--- Score

88. What actually has to improve and by how much?
<--- Score

89. How will you know that a change is an improvement?
<--- Score

90. Do vendor agreements bring new compliance risk ?
<--- Score

91. What is Safety management systems's impact on utilizing the best solution(s)?
<--- Score

92. How do you improve your likelihood of success ?
<--- Score

93. What to do with the results or outcomes of measurements?
<--- Score

94. How do you measure risk?
<--- Score

95. What are your current levels and trends in key measures or indicators of workforce and leader development?

<--- Score

96. How scalable is your Safety management systems solution?
<--- Score

97. Can you integrate quality management and risk management?
<--- Score

98. Is the measure of success for Safety management systems understandable to a variety of people?
<--- Score

99. Is the Safety management systems documentation thorough?
<--- Score

100. Risk Identification: What are the possible risk events your organization faces in relation to Safety management systems?
<--- Score

101. How do the Safety management systems results compare with the performance of your competitors and other organizations with similar offerings?
<--- Score

102. What Safety management systems improvements can be made?
<--- Score

103. How are Safety management systems risks managed?
<--- Score

104. What is Safety management systems risk?
<--- Score

105. How does your organization evaluate strategic Safety management systems success?
<--- Score

106. What tools were used to tap into the creativity and encourage 'outside the box' thinking?
<--- Score

107. Where do you need Safety management systems improvement?
<--- Score

108. At what point will vulnerability assessments be performed once Safety management systems is put into production (e.g., ongoing Risk Management after implementation)?
<--- Score

109. How can the phases of Safety management systems development be identified?
<--- Score

110. Do you combine technical expertise with business knowledge and Safety management systems Key topics include lifecycles, development approaches, requirements and how to make a business case?
<--- Score

111. How do you measure progress and evaluate training effectiveness?
<--- Score

112. What is the Safety management systems's sustainability risk?
<--- Score

113. What are the Safety management systems security risks?
<--- Score

114. Is supporting Safety management systems documentation required?
<--- Score

115. Is Safety management systems documentation maintained?
<--- Score

116. Who are the Safety management systems decision-makers?
<--- Score

117. What can you do to improve?
<--- Score

118. What alternative responses are available to manage risk?
<--- Score

119. Who should make the Safety management systems decisions?
<--- Score

120. How can you improve performance?
<--- Score

121. Why improve in the first place?
<--- Score

122. Will the controls trigger any other risks?
<--- Score

123. Where do the Safety management systems decisions reside?
<--- Score

124. Can the solution be designed and implemented within an acceptable time period?
<--- Score

125. Is risk periodically assessed?
<--- Score

126. What is the magnitude of the improvements?
<--- Score

127. Do those selected for the Safety management systems team have a good general understanding of what Safety management systems is all about?
<--- Score

128. How significant is the improvement in the eyes of the end user?
<--- Score

129. How is continuous improvement applied to risk management?
<--- Score

130. To what extent does management recognize Safety management systems as a tool to increase the results?
<--- Score

131. How do you manage Safety management systems risk?
<--- Score

132. Who are the key stakeholders for the Safety management systems evaluation?
<--- Score

133. Who controls the risk?
<--- Score

134. What is the implementation plan?
<--- Score

135. Risk factors: what are the characteristics of Safety management systems that make it risky?
<--- Score

136. What assumptions are made about the solution and approach?
<--- Score

Add up total points for this section:
_ _ _ _ _ = Total points for this section

Divided by: _ _ _ _ _ _ (number of statements answered) = _ _ _ _ _ _
Average score for this section

Transfer your score to the Safety management systems Index at the beginning of the Self-Assessment.

CRITERION #6: CONTROL:

INTENT: Implement the practical solution. Maintain the performance and correct possible complications.

In my belief, the answer to this question is clearly defined:

5 Strongly Agree

4 Agree

3 Neutral

2 Disagree

1 Strongly Disagree

1. How do you encourage people to take control and responsibility?
<--- Score

2. How will Safety management systems decisions be made and monitored?
<--- Score

3. Will the team be available to assist members in

planning investigations?
<--- Score

4. How do you select, collect, align, and integrate Safety management systems data and information for tracking daily operations and overall organizational performance, including progress relative to strategic objectives and action plans?
<--- Score

5. How widespread is its use?
<--- Score

6. In the case of a Safety management systems project, the criteria for the audit derive from implementation objectives, an audit of a Safety management systems project involves assessing whether the recommendations outlined for implementation have been met, can you track that any Safety management systems project is implemented as planned, and is it working?
<--- Score

7. Is a response plan in place for when the input, process, or output measures indicate an 'out-of-control' condition?
<--- Score

8. Will any special training be provided for results interpretation?
<--- Score

9. How will new or emerging customer needs/ requirements be checked/communicated to orient the process toward meeting the new specifications and continually reducing variation?

<--- Score

10. Do the viable solutions scale to future needs?
<--- Score

11. How likely is the current Safety management systems plan to come in on schedule or on budget?
<--- Score

12. What Safety management systems standards are applicable?
<--- Score

13. What are the performance and scale of the Safety management systems tools?
<--- Score

14. Is there a recommended audit plan for routine surveillance inspections of Safety management systems's gains?
<--- Score

15. Has the Safety management systems value of standards been quantified?
<--- Score

16. Is new knowledge gained imbedded in the response plan?
<--- Score

17. What key inputs and outputs are being measured on an ongoing basis?
<--- Score

18. How will the day-to-day responsibilities for monitoring and continual improvement be

transferred from the improvement team to the process owner?
<--- Score

19. How do you plan on providing proper recognition and disclosure of supporting companies?
<--- Score

20. How will report readings be checked to effectively monitor performance?
<--- Score

21. What other areas of the group might benefit from the Safety management systems team's improvements, knowledge, and learning?
<--- Score

22. Are suggested corrective/restorative actions indicated on the response plan for known causes to problems that might surface?
<--- Score

23. Is reporting being used or needed?
<--- Score

24. How will you measure your QA plan's effectiveness?
<--- Score

25. How will the process owner and team be able to hold the gains?
<--- Score

26. What are customers monitoring?
<--- Score

27. Will your goals reflect your program budget?
<--- Score

28. Who has control over resources?
<--- Score

29. Implementation Planning: is a pilot needed to test the changes before a full roll out occurs?
<--- Score

30. What is the standard for acceptable Safety management systems performance?
<--- Score

31. Do you monitor the Safety management systems decisions made and fine tune them as they evolve?
<--- Score

32. Are operating procedures consistent?
<--- Score

33. What adjustments to the strategies are needed?
<--- Score

34. Is there a documented and implemented monitoring plan?
<--- Score

35. What are you attempting to measure/monitor?
<--- Score

36. Does job training on the documented procedures need to be part of the process team's education and training?
<--- Score

37. What should the next improvement project be that is related to Safety management systems?
<--- Score

38. Are the planned controls in place?
<--- Score

39. How do your controls stack up?
<--- Score

40. Can support from partners be adjusted?
<--- Score

41. Does Safety management systems appropriately measure and monitor risk?
<--- Score

42. What is your plan to assess your security risks?
<--- Score

43. What quality tools were useful in the control phase?
<--- Score

44. How do controls support value?
<--- Score

45. Are new process steps, standards, and documentation ingrained into normal operations?
<--- Score

46. How will input, process, and output variables be checked to detect for sub-optimal conditions?
<--- Score

47. Are controls in place and consistently applied?

<--- Score

48. What can you control?
<--- Score

49. What are the key elements of your Safety management systems performance improvement system, including your evaluation, organizational learning, and innovation processes?
<--- Score

50. What do you measure to verify effectiveness gains?
<--- Score

51. How do you spread information?
<--- Score

52. Is there a Safety management systems Communication plan covering who needs to get what information when?
<--- Score

53. Are the planned controls working?
<--- Score

54. Is there a standardized process?
<--- Score

55. Against what alternative is success being measured?
<--- Score

56. Will existing staff require re-training, for example, to learn new business processes?
<--- Score

57. Are you measuring, monitoring and predicting Safety management systems activities to optimize operations and profitability, and enhancing outcomes?
<--- Score

58. Does the Safety management systems performance meet the customer's requirements?
<--- Score

59. How might the group capture best practices and lessons learned so as to leverage improvements?
<--- Score

60. What is the best design framework for Safety management systems organization now that, in a post industrial-age if the top-down, command and control model is no longer relevant?
<--- Score

61. What is the recommended frequency of auditing?
<--- Score

62. Is knowledge gained on process shared and institutionalized?
<--- Score

63. How will the process owner verify improvement in present and future sigma levels, process capabilities?
<--- Score

64. Does a troubleshooting guide exist or is it needed?
<--- Score

65. Is there documentation that will support the

successful operation of the improvement?
<--- Score

66. How do you establish and deploy modified action plans if circumstances require a shift in plans and rapid execution of new plans?
<--- Score

67. How is Safety management systems project cost planned, managed, monitored?
<--- Score

68. What is the control/monitoring plan?
<--- Score

69. What should you measure to verify efficiency gains?
<--- Score

70. Is there an action plan in case of emergencies?
<--- Score

71. Are pertinent alerts monitored, analyzed and distributed to appropriate personnel?
<--- Score

72. Are there documented procedures?
<--- Score

73. Are documented procedures clear and easy to follow for the operators?
<--- Score

74. Is a response plan established and deployed?
<--- Score

75. Has the improved process and its steps been standardized?
<--- Score

76. Do you monitor the effectiveness of your Safety management systems activities?
<--- Score

77. Have new or revised work instructions resulted?
<--- Score

78. Is the Safety management systems test/monitoring cost justified?
<--- Score

79. What are your results for key measures or indicators of the accomplishment of your Safety management systems strategy and action plans, including building and strengthening core competencies?
<--- Score

80. Are the Safety management systems standards challenging?
<--- Score

81. What other systems, operations, processes, and infrastructures (hiring practices, staffing, training, incentives/rewards, metrics/dashboards/scorecards, etc.) need updates, additions, changes, or deletions in order to facilitate knowledge transfer and improvements?
<--- Score

82. Is there a control plan in place for sustaining improvements (short and long-term)?

<--- Score

83. You may have created your quality measures at a time when you lacked resources, technology wasn't up to the required standard, or low service levels were the industry norm. Have those circumstances changed?
<--- Score

84. Who controls critical resources?
<--- Score

85. Is there a transfer of ownership and knowledge to process owner and process team tasked with the responsibilities.
<--- Score

86. Who is the Safety management systems process owner?
<--- Score

87. Who sets the Safety management systems standards?
<--- Score

88. What are the critical parameters to watch?
<--- Score

89. How do senior leaders actions reflect a commitment to the organizations Safety management systems values?
<--- Score

90. How is change control managed?
<--- Score

91. Act/Adjust: What Do you Need to Do Differently?
<--- Score

92. How can you best use all of your knowledge repositories to enhance learning and sharing?
<--- Score

93. Who is going to spread your message?
<--- Score

94. Do the Safety management systems decisions you make today help people and the planet tomorrow?
<--- Score

95. What is your theory of human motivation, and how does your compensation plan fit with that view?
<--- Score

96. What do you stand for--and what are you against?
<--- Score

97. How do you plan for the cost of succession?
<--- Score

98. Can you adapt and adjust to changing Safety management systems situations?
<--- Score

99. Does the response plan contain a definite closed loop continual improvement scheme (e.g., plan-do-check-act)?
<--- Score

Add up total points for this section:
_ _ _ _ _ = Total points for this section

Divided by: _____ (number of
statements answered) = _____
Average score for this section

Transfer your score to the Safety
management systems Index at the
beginning of the Self-Assessment.

CRITERION #7: SUSTAIN:

INTENT: Retain the benefits.

In my belief, the answer to this
question is clearly defined:

5 Strongly Agree

4 Agree

3 Neutral

2 Disagree

1 Strongly Disagree

1. At what moment would you think; Will I get fired?
<--- Score

2. How will you ensure you get what you expected?
<--- Score

3. What is the source of the strategies for Safety
management systems strengthening and reform?
<--- Score

4. What is your competitive advantage?

<--- Score

5. Where can you break convention?
<--- Score

6. How will you insure seamless interoperability of Safety management systems moving forward?
<--- Score

7. What have you done to protect your business from competitive encroachment?
<--- Score

8. How do you make it meaningful in connecting Safety management systems with what users do day-to-day?
<--- Score

9. Do you have an implicit bias for capital investments over people investments?
<--- Score

10. How do you foster innovation?
<--- Score

11. Why is it important to have senior management support for a Safety management systems project?
<--- Score

12. What are you challenging?
<--- Score

13. Which Safety management systems goals are the most important?
<--- Score

14. How much does Safety management systems help?
<--- Score

15. What is the estimated value of the project?
<--- Score

16. Is your strategy driving your strategy? Or is the way in which you allocate resources driving your strategy?
<--- Score

17. How do you create buy-in?
<--- Score

18. Are your responses positive or negative?
<--- Score

19. Do you have the right people on the bus?
<--- Score

20. How do customers see your organization?
<--- Score

21. What are your personal philosophies regarding Safety management systems and how do they influence your work?
<--- Score

22. What is something you believe that nearly no one agrees with you on?
<--- Score

23. Marketing budgets are tighter, consumers are more skeptical, and social media has changed forever the way we talk about Safety management systems,

how do you gain traction?
<--- Score

24. How important is Safety management systems to the user organizations mission?
<--- Score

25. Is it economical; do you have the time and money?
<--- Score

26. Do you have past Safety management systems successes?
<--- Score

27. How do you accomplish your long range Safety management systems goals?
<--- Score

28. What unique value proposition (UVP) do you offer?
<--- Score

29. What may be the consequences for the performance of an organization if all stakeholders are not consulted regarding Safety management systems?
<--- Score

30. What is your formula for success in Safety management systems ?
<--- Score

31. If there were zero limitations, what would you do differently?
<--- Score

32. What knowledge, skills and characteristics mark a

good Safety management systems project manager?
<--- Score

33. How do concepts or initiatives relate to food safety management systems?
<--- Score

34. Is a Safety management systems breakthrough on the horizon?
<--- Score

35. What will be the consequences to the stakeholder (financial, reputation etc) if Safety management systems does not go ahead or fails to deliver the objectives?
<--- Score

36. Do you know what you are doing? And who do you call if you don't?
<--- Score

37. What is the overall business strategy?
<--- Score

38. What is your BATNA (best alternative to a negotiated agreement)?
<--- Score

39. Is Safety management systems dependent on the successful delivery of a current project?
<--- Score

40. Would you rather sell to knowledgeable and informed customers or to uninformed customers?
<--- Score

41. If you had to leave your organization for a year and the only communication you could have with employees/colleagues was a single paragraph, what would you write?
<--- Score

42. Whom among your colleagues do you trust, and for what?
<--- Score

43. How do you assess the Safety management systems pitfalls that are inherent in implementing it?
<--- Score

44. Why should people listen to you?
<--- Score

45. Are the criteria for selecting recommendations stated?
<--- Score

46. Is there any existing Safety management systems governance structure?
<--- Score

47. Are the assumptions believable and achievable?
<--- Score

48. What do we do when new problems arise?
<--- Score

49. Has implementation been effective in reaching specified objectives so far?
<--- Score

50. What projects are going on in the organization

today, and what resources are those projects using from the resource pools?
<--- Score

51. Are you maintaining a past–present–future perspective throughout the Safety management systems discussion?
<--- Score

52. Can you break it down?
<--- Score

53. What happens at your organization when people fail?
<--- Score

54. How will you know that the Safety management systems project has been successful?
<--- Score

55. What potential megatrends could make your business model obsolete?
<--- Score

56. Who else should you help?
<--- Score

57. What threat is Safety management systems addressing?
<--- Score

58. Who do you want your customers to become?
<--- Score

59. What goals did you miss?
<--- Score

60. Whose voice (department, ethnic group, women, older workers, etc) might you have missed hearing from in your company, and how might you amplify this voice to create positive momentum for your business?
<--- Score

61. How are you doing compared to your industry?
<--- Score

62. Is Safety management systems realistic, or are you setting yourself up for failure?
<--- Score

63. Who is responsible for errors?
<--- Score

64. Who, on the executive team or the board, has spoken to a customer recently?
<--- Score

65. How do you ensure that implementations of Safety management systems products are done in a way that ensures safety?
<--- Score

66. What are internal and external Safety management systems relations?
<--- Score

67. Who is responsible for ensuring appropriate resources (time, people and money) are allocated to Safety management systems?
<--- Score

68. Do you have enough freaky customers in your portfolio pushing you to the limit day in and day out?
<--- Score

69. Why not do Safety management systems?
<--- Score

70. Who is responsible for Safety management systems?
<--- Score

71. What does your signature ensure?
<--- Score

72. How do you go about securing Safety management systems?
<--- Score

73. Why will customers want to buy your organizations products/services?
<--- Score

74. What stupid rule would you most like to kill?
<--- Score

75. What are the long-term Safety management systems goals?
<--- Score

76. How do senior leaders deploy your organizations vision and values through your leadership system, to the workforce, to key suppliers and partners, and to customers and other stakeholders, as appropriate?
<--- Score

77. What role does communication play in the success

or failure of a Safety management systems project?
<--- Score

78. Are you satisfied with your current role? If not, what is missing from it?
<--- Score

79. Do you see more potential in people than they do in themselves?
<--- Score

80. Will it be accepted by users?
<--- Score

81. Do you think Safety management systems accomplishes the goals you expect it to accomplish?
<--- Score

82. What business benefits will Safety management systems goals deliver if achieved?
<--- Score

83. Are all key stakeholders present at all Structured Walkthroughs?
<--- Score

84. Do you know who is a friend or a foe?
<--- Score

85. Are assumptions made in Safety management systems stated explicitly?
<--- Score

86. Do Safety management systems rules make a reasonable demand on a users capabilities?
<--- Score

87. What counts that you are not counting?
<--- Score

88. What is an unauthorized commitment?
<--- Score

89. If no one would ever find out about your accomplishments, how would you lead differently?
<--- Score

90. Is there a work around that you can use?
<--- Score

91. What is it like to work for you?
<--- Score

92. Do you say no to customers for no reason?
<--- Score

93. What Safety management systems modifications can you make work for you?
<--- Score

94. Political -is anyone trying to undermine this project?
<--- Score

95. How is implementation research currently incorporated into each of your goals?
<--- Score

96. Who is on the team?
<--- Score

97. What are the gaps in your knowledge and

experience?
<--- Score

98. What relationships among Safety management systems trends do you perceive?
<--- Score

99. Have benefits been optimized with all key stakeholders?
<--- Score

100. Why is Safety management systems important for you now?
<--- Score

101. How do you engage the workforce, in addition to satisfying them?
<--- Score

102. If you had to rebuild your organization without any traditional competitive advantages (i.e., no killer technology, promising research, innovative product/ service delivery model, etcetera), how would your people have to approach their work and collaborate together in order to create the necessary conditions for success?
<--- Score

103. How can you incorporate support to ensure safe and effective use of Safety management systems into the services that you provide?
<--- Score

104. If you were responsible for initiating and implementing major changes in your organization, what steps might you take to ensure acceptance of

those changes?
<--- Score

105. How can you become the company that would put you out of business?
<--- Score

106. What is the purpose of Safety management systems in relation to the mission?
<--- Score

107. How does Safety management systems integrate with other stakeholder initiatives?
<--- Score

108. Are you paying enough attention to the partners your company depends on to succeed?
<--- Score

109. How do you listen to customers to obtain actionable information?
<--- Score

110. What must you excel at?
<--- Score

111. What you are going to do to affect the numbers?
<--- Score

112. How do you know if you are successful?
<--- Score

113. What happens when a new employee joins the organization?
<--- Score

114. How likely is it that a customer would recommend your company to a friend or colleague?
<--- Score

115. What trophy do you want on your mantle?
<--- Score

116. Is a Safety management systems team work effort in place?
<--- Score

117. How do you maintain Safety management systems's Integrity?
<--- Score

118. What trouble can you get into?
<--- Score

119. Think of your Safety management systems project, what are the main functions?
<--- Score

120. Operational - will it work?
<--- Score

121. Who uses your product in ways you never expected?
<--- Score

122. What is your question? Why?
<--- Score

123. How do you track customer value, profitability or financial return, organizational success, and sustainability?
<--- Score

124. How do you set Safety management systems stretch targets and how do you get people to not only participate in setting these stretch targets but also that they strive to achieve these?
<--- Score

125. If your customer were your grandmother, would you tell her to buy what you're selling?
<--- Score

126. What have been your experiences in defining long range Safety management systems goals?
<--- Score

127. Who do you think the world wants your organization to be?
<--- Score

128. How do you govern and fulfill your societal responsibilities?
<--- Score

129. What happens if you do not have enough funding?
<--- Score

130. What was the last experiment you ran?
<--- Score

131. What are the essentials of internal Safety management systems management?
<--- Score

132. Are there any activities that you can take off your to do list?

<--- Score

133. If you find that you havent accomplished one of the goals for one of the steps of the Safety management systems strategy, what will you do to fix it?
<--- Score

134. What is the funding source for this project?
<--- Score

135. How do you provide a safe environment -physically and emotionally?
<--- Score

136. What management system can you use to leverage the Safety management systems experience, ideas, and concerns of the people closest to the work to be done?
<--- Score

137. Is the Safety management systems organization completing tasks effectively and efficiently?
<--- Score

138. How well do the Safety Management Systems compare?
<--- Score

139. How much contingency will be available in the budget?
<--- Score

140. How can you negotiate Safety management systems successfully with a stubborn boss, an irate client, or a deceitful coworker?

<--- Score

141. Can the schedule be done in the given time?
<--- Score

142. What would have to be true for the option on the table to be the best possible choice?
<--- Score

143. To whom do you add value?
<--- Score

144. What are the usability implications of Safety management systems actions?
<--- Score

145. Are you changing as fast as the world around you?
<--- Score

146. Who are your customers?
<--- Score

147. Are you using a design thinking approach and integrating Innovation, Safety management systems Experience, and Brand Value?
<--- Score

148. Is your basic point _____ or _____?
<--- Score

149. Who have you, as a company, historically been when you've been at your best?
<--- Score

150. What is a feasible sequencing of reform initiatives

over time?
<--- Score

151. Are you making progress, and are you making progress as Safety management systems leaders?
<--- Score

152. Are you relevant? Will you be relevant five years from now? Ten?
<--- Score

153. What are the business goals Safety management systems is aiming to achieve?
<--- Score

154. What new services of functionality will be implemented next with Safety management systems ?
<--- Score

155. Who will determine interim and final deadlines?
<--- Score

156. What are current Safety management systems paradigms?
<--- Score

157. How do you lead with Safety management systems in mind?
<--- Score

158. Have new benefits been realized?
<--- Score

159. Is the impact that Safety management systems has shown?

<--- Score

160. How do you determine the key elements that affect Safety management systems workforce satisfaction, how are these elements determined for different workforce groups and segments?
<--- Score

161. Who will be responsible for deciding whether Safety management systems goes ahead or not after the initial investigations?
<--- Score

162. How do you keep the momentum going?
<--- Score

163. What are the success criteria that will indicate that Safety management systems objectives have been met and the benefits delivered?
<--- Score

164. How will you motivate the stakeholders with the least vested interest?
<--- Score

165. Who are the key stakeholders?
<--- Score

166. What is the kind of project structure that would be appropriate for your Safety management systems project, should it be formal and complex, or can it be less formal and relatively simple?
<--- Score

167. What one word do you want to own in the minds of your customers, employees, and partners?

<--- Score

168. What are the potential basics of Safety management systems fraud?
<--- Score

169. What are the key enablers to make this Safety management systems move?
<--- Score

170. Ask yourself: how would you do this work if you only had one staff member to do it?
<--- Score

171. What are the top 3 things at the forefront of your Safety management systems agendas for the next 3 years?
<--- Score

172. What is your Safety management systems strategy?
<--- Score

173. If your company went out of business tomorrow, would anyone who doesn't get a paycheck here care?
<--- Score

174. In a project to restructure Safety management systems outcomes, which stakeholders would you involve?
<--- Score

175. What did you miss in the interview for the worst hire you ever made?
<--- Score

176. What Safety management systems skills are most important?
<--- Score

177. Do you have the right capabilities and capacities?
<--- Score

178. In retrospect, of the projects that you pulled the plug on, what percent do you wish had been allowed to keep going, and what percent do you wish had ended earlier?
<--- Score

179. What is the craziest thing you can do?
<--- Score

180. Why do and why don't your customers like your organization?
<--- Score

181. How long will it take to change?
<--- Score

182. Is there any reason to believe the opposite of my current belief?
<--- Score

183. What are the challenges?
<--- Score

184. How do you foster the skills, knowledge, talents, attributes, and characteristics you want to have?
<--- Score

185. What are the rules and assumptions your industry operates under? What if the opposite were true?

<--- Score

186. If you weren't already in this business, would you enter it today? And if not, what are you going to do about it?
<--- Score

187. What should you stop doing?
<--- Score

188. Instead of going to current contacts for new ideas, what if you reconnected with dormant contacts--the people you used to know? If you were going reactivate a dormant tie, who would it be?
<--- Score

189. Can you do all this work?
<--- Score

190. Which individuals, teams or departments will be involved in Safety management systems?
<--- Score

191. How can you become more high-tech but still be high touch?
<--- Score

192. Are new benefits received and understood?
<--- Score

193. If you do not follow, then how to lead?
<--- Score

194. How do you stay inspired?
<--- Score

195. How do you manage Safety management systems Knowledge Management (KM)?
<--- Score

196. Are you / should you be revolutionary or evolutionary?
<--- Score

197. What is the recommended frequency of auditing?
<--- Score

198. What is the range of capabilities?
<--- Score

199. How do you keep records, of what?
<--- Score

200. Which models, tools and techniques are necessary?
<--- Score

201. What tools do you use once you have decided on a Safety management systems strategy and more importantly how do you choose?
<--- Score

202. How do you deal with Safety management systems changes?
<--- Score

203. What information is critical to your organization that your executives are ignoring?
<--- Score

204. Why should you adopt a Safety management systems framework?

<--- Score

205. Will there be any necessary staff changes (redundancies or new hires)?
<--- Score

206. What is the big Safety management systems idea?
<--- Score

207. Did your employees make progress today?
<--- Score

208. What is effective Safety management systems?
<--- Score

209. In the past year, what have you done (or could you have done) to increase the accurate perception of your company/brand as ethical and honest?
<--- Score

210. Were lessons learned captured and communicated?
<--- Score

211. What are specific Safety management systems rules to follow?
<--- Score

212. What are you trying to prove to yourself, and how might it be hijacking your life and business success?
<--- Score

213. Who are four people whose careers you have enhanced?
<--- Score

214. What is the overall talent health of your organization as a whole at senior levels, and for each organization reporting to a member of the Senior Leadership Team?
<--- Score

215. Who will manage the integration of tools?
<--- Score

216. What could happen if you do not do it?
<--- Score

217. Which functions and people interact with the supplier and or customer?
<--- Score

218. Do you feel that more should be done in the Safety management systems area?
<--- Score

Add up total points for this section:
_ _ _ _ _ = Total points for this section

Divided by: _ _ _ _ _ _ (number of statements answered) = _ _ _ _ _ _
Average score for this section

Transfer your score to the Safety management systems Index at the beginning of the Self-Assessment.

Safety Management Systems and Managing Projects, Criteria for Project Managers:

1.0 Initiating Process Group: Safety Management Systems

1. When must it be done?

2. How is each deliverable reviewed, verified, and validated?

3. What are the inputs required to produce the deliverables?

4. When are the deliverables to be generated in each phase?

5. At which cmmi level are software processes documented, standardized, and integrated into a standard to-be practiced process for your organization?

6. Mitigate. what will you do to minimize the impact should the risk event occur?

7. Who is funding the Safety Management Systems project?

8. Do you understand all business (operational), technical, resource and vendor risks associated with the Safety Management Systems project?

9. What were the challenges that you encountered during the execution of a previous Safety Management Systems project that you would not want to repeat?

10. Who is performing the work of the Safety

Management Systems project?

11. The process to Manage Stakeholders is part of which process group?

12. Although the Safety Management Systems project manager does not directly manage procurement and contracting activities, who does manage procurement and contracting activities in your organization then if not the PM?

13. Does it make any difference if you am successful?

14. Which of six sigmas dmaic phases focuses on the measurement of internal process that affect factors that are critical to quality?

15. What are the overarching issues of your organization?

16. Are the changes in your Safety Management Systems project being formally requested, analyzed, and approved by the appropriate decision makers?

17. Are the Safety Management Systems project team and stakeholders meeting regularly and using a meeting agenda and taking notes to accurately document what is being covered and what happened in the weekly meetings?

18. Are there resources to maintain and support the outcome of the Safety Management Systems project?

19. How well did you do?

20. Who supports, improves, and oversees

standardized processes related to the Safety Management Systems projects program?

1.1 Project Charter: Safety Management Systems

21. Who is the Safety Management Systems project Manager?

22. Why do you manage integration?

23. Who will take notes, document decisions?

24. Who is the sponsor?

25. What ideas do you have for initial tests of change (PDSA cycles)?

26. Are you building in-house ?

27. Major high-level milestone targets: what events measure progress?

28. Customer benefits: what customer requirements does this Safety Management Systems project address?

29. Run it as as a startup?

30. How will you know that a change is an improvement?

31. Environmental stewardship and sustainability considerations: what is the process that will be used to ensure compliance with the environmental stewardship policy?

32. When do you use a Safety Management Systems project Charter?

33. What does it need to do?

34. What outcome, in measureable terms, are you hoping to accomplish?

35. Who manages integration?

36. Does the Safety Management Systems project need to consider any special capacity or capability issues?

37. Strategic fit: what is the strategic initiative identifier for this Safety Management Systems project?

38. Why do you need to manage scope?

39. Must Have?

40. Did your Safety Management Systems project ask for this?

1.2 Stakeholder Register: Safety Management Systems

41. Who wants to talk about Security?

42. How much influence do they have on the Safety Management Systems project?

43. How big is the gap?

44. Who are the stakeholders?

45. What & Why?

46. How will reports be created?

47. What opportunities exist to provide communications?

48. Who is managing stakeholder engagement?

49. What is the power of the stakeholder?

50. Is your organization ready for change?

51. How should employers make voices heard?

52. What are the major Safety Management Systems project milestones requiring communications or providing communications opportunities?

1.3 Stakeholder Analysis Matrix: Safety Management Systems

53. Management cover, succession?

54. How does the Safety Management Systems project involve consultations or collaboration with other organizations?

55. Continuity, supply chain robustness?

56. Who will be affected by the work?

57. Global influences?

58. What unique or lowest-cost resources does the Safety Management Systems project have access to?

59. It developments?

60. What is the stakeholders power and status in relation to the Safety Management Systems project?

61. Is there evidence that demonstrates the impact of education on the Safety Management Systems projects outcomes?

62. Which conditions out of the control of the management are crucial for the sustainability of its effects?

63. What are innovative aspects of your organization?

64. Who determines value?

65. What is the range you need to look at?

66. How to measure the achievement of the Immediate Objective?

67. Morale, commitment, leadership?

68. Who will promote/support the Safety Management Systems project, provided that they are involved?

69. What is the issue at stake?

70. Technology development and innovation?

71. Financial reserves, likely returns?

72. Identify the stakeholders levels most frequently used –or at least sought– in your Safety Management Systems projects and for which purpose?

2.0 Planning Process Group: Safety Management Systems

73. You are creating your WBS and find that you keep decomposing tasks into smaller and smaller units. How can you tell when you are done?

74. To what extent have the target population and participants made the activities own, taking an active role in it?

75. What types of differentiated effects are resulting from the Safety Management Systems project and to what extent?

76. What is involved in Safety Management Systems project scope management, and why is good Safety Management Systems project scope management so important on information technology Safety Management Systems projects?

77. Just how important is your work to the overall success of the Safety Management Systems project?

78. How can you tell when you are done?

79. What do you need to do?

80. Why do it Safety Management Systems projects fail?

81. To what extent do the intervention objectives and strategies of the Safety Management Systems project

respond to your organizations plans?

82. How are it Safety Management Systems projects different?

83. If a task is partitionable, is this a sufficient condition to reduce the Safety Management Systems project duration?

84. How will it affect you?

85. How can you make your needs known?

86. Have more efficient (sensitive) and appropriate measures been adopted to respond to the political and socio-cultural problems identified?

87. When will the Safety Management Systems project be done?

88. Will you be replaced?

89. How well do the team follow the chosen processes?

90. Have operating capacities been created and/or reinforced in partners?

91. To what extent and in what ways are the Safety Management Systems project contributing to progress towards organizational reform?

92. How should needs be met?

2.1 Project Management Plan: Safety Management Systems

93. Is the budget realistic?

94. Does the implementation plan have an appropriate division of responsibilities?

95. When is the Safety Management Systems project management plan created?

96. Development trends and opportunities. What if the positive direction and vision of your organization causes expected trends to change?

97. Was the peer (technical) review of the cost estimates duly coordinated with the cost estimate center of expertise and addressed in the review documentation and certification?

98. Do there need to be organizational changes?

99. What data/reports/tools/etc. do program managers need?

100. What are the assigned resources?

101. Are calculations and results of analyzes essentially correct?

102. What did not work so well?

103. Do the proposed changes from the Safety

Management Systems project include any significant risks to safety?

104. Is the engineering content at a feasibility level-of-detail, and is it sufficiently complete, to provide an adequate basis for the baseline cost estimate?

105. Are comparable cost estimates used for comparing, screening and selecting alternative plans, and has a reasonable cost estimate been developed for the recommended plan?

106. What is risk management?

107. What worked well?

108. What is the justification?

109. Is there an incremental analysis/cost effectiveness analysis of proposed mitigation features based on an approved method and using an accepted model?

110. If the Safety Management Systems project management plan is a comprehensive document that guides you in Safety Management Systems project execution and control, then what should it NOT contain?

111. Does the selected plan protect privacy?

112. What if, for example, the positive direction and vision of your organization causes expected trends to change resulting in greater need than expected?

2.2 Scope Management Plan: Safety Management Systems

113. What are the acceptance criteria (process and criteria to be met for key stakeholder acceptance) and who is authorized to sign off?

114. Has process improvement efforts been completed before requirements efforts begin?

115. Organizational policies that might affect the availability of resources?

116. Are you doing what you have set out to do?

117. What if you do not have more detailed information on the report?

118. How much money have you spent?

119. Are risk triggers captured?

120. Are meeting minutes captured and sent out after the meeting?

121. How many changes are you making?

122. What are the risks that could significantly affect the budget of the Safety Management Systems project?

123. Are post milestone Safety Management Systems project reviews (PMPR) conducted with your

organization at least once a year?

124. What weaknesses do you have?

125. What went right?

126. How relevant is this attribute to this Safety Management Systems project or audit?

127. Have stakeholder accountabilities & responsibilities been clearly defined?

128. Is the Safety Management Systems project status reviewed with the steering and executive teams at appropriate intervals?

129. Are schedule deliverables actually delivered?

130. Are the quality tools and methods identified in the Quality Plan appropriate to the Safety Management Systems project?

131. Have all necessary approvals been obtained?

2.3 Requirements Management Plan: Safety Management Systems

132. How knowledgeable is the team in the proposed application area?

133. Do you expect stakeholders to be cooperative?

134. Who will finally present the work or product(s) for acceptance?

135. Should you include sub-activities?

136. Are actual resources expenditures versus planned expenditures acceptable?

137. What are you counting on?

138. When and how will a requirements baseline be established in this Safety Management Systems project?

139. Subject to change control?

140. What cost metrics will be used?

141. The wbs is developed as part of a joint planning session. and how do you know that youhave done this right?

142. In case of software development; Should you have a test for each code module?

143. Is infrastructure setup part of your Safety Management Systems project?

144. Will you have access to stakeholders when you need them?

145. Who is responsible for monitoring and tracking the Safety Management Systems project requirements?

146. Who is responsible for quantifying the Safety Management Systems project requirements?

147. Who will do the reporting and to whom will reports be delivered?

148. How detailed should the Safety Management Systems project get?

149. Do you understand the role that each stakeholder will play in the requirements process?

150. How will the information be distributed?

2.4 Requirements Documentation: Safety Management Systems

151. How linear / iterative is your Requirements Gathering process (or will it be)?

152. How does the proposed Safety Management Systems project contribute to the overall objectives of your organization?

153. What happens when requirements are wrong?

154. Do technical resources exist?

155. How much testing do you need to do to prove that your system is safe?

156. Is new technology needed?

157. Has requirements gathering uncovered information that would necessitate changes?

158. Does your organization restrict technical alternatives?

159. How can you document system requirements?

160. How to document system requirements?

161. What are the acceptance criteria?

162. What kind of entity is a problem ?

163. Is your business case still valid?

164. What is effective documentation?

165. Can the requirements be checked?

166. Where do system and software requirements come from, what are sources?

167. Is the requirement properly understood?

168. Can the requirement be changed without a large impact on other requirements?

169. How much does requirements engineering cost?

170. What images does it conjure?

2.5 Requirements Traceability Matrix: Safety Management Systems

171. What are the chronologies, contingencies, consequences, criteria?

172. Why use a WBS?

173. How will it affect the stakeholders personally in career?

174. Describe the process for approving requirements so they can be added to the traceability matrix and Safety Management Systems project work can be performed. Will the Safety Management Systems project requirements become approved in writing?

175. What percentage of Safety Management Systems projects are producing traceability matrices between requirements and other work products?

176. Do you have a clear understanding of all subcontracts in place?

177. Why do you manage scope?

178. Will you use a Requirements Traceability Matrix?

179. How small is small enough?

180. What is the WBS?

181. How do you manage scope?

182. Is there a requirements traceability process in place?

2.6 Project Scope Statement: Safety Management Systems

183. Relevant - ask yourself can you get there; why are you doing this Safety Management Systems project?

184. Will there be a Change Control Process in place?

185. Are the input requirements from the team members clearly documented and communicated?

186. Have the configuration management functions been assigned?

187. Will all tasks resulting from issues be entered into the Safety Management Systems project Plan and tracked through the plan?

188. What are the major deliverables of the Safety Management Systems project?

189. If there are vendors, have they signed off on the Safety Management Systems project Plan?

190. Will this process be communicated to the customer and Safety Management Systems project team?

191. Is the Safety Management Systems project organization documented and on file?

192. Is the scope of your Safety Management Systems project well defined?

193. Is the Safety Management Systems project sponsor function identified and defined?

194. Is this process communicated to the customer and team members?

195. Has everyone approved the Safety Management Systems projects scope statement?

196. What is the most common tool for helping define the detail?

197. Elements of scope management that deal with concept development ?

198. Write a brief purpose statement for this Safety Management Systems project. Include a business justification statement. What is the product of this Safety Management Systems project?

199. Once its defined, what is the stability of the Safety Management Systems project scope?

200. What actions will be taken to mitigate the risk?

201. Were potential customers involved early in the planning process?

2.7 Assumption and Constraint Log: Safety Management Systems

202. Have adequate resources been provided by management to ensure Safety Management Systems project success?

203. If appropriate, is the deliverable content consistent with current Safety Management Systems project documents and in compliance with the Document Management Plan?

204. Does the document/deliverable meet all requirements (for example, statement of work) specific to this deliverable?

205. Does the system design reflect the requirements?

206. Have all stakeholders been identified?

207. Do the requirements meet the standards of correctness, completeness, consistency, accuracy, and readability?

208. Has the approach and development strategy of the Safety Management Systems project been defined, documented and accepted by the appropriate stakeholders?

209. How many Safety Management Systems project staff does this specific process affect?

210. Were the system requirements formally reviewed

prior to initiating the design phase?

211. Do you know what your customers expectations are regarding this process?

212. Is the current scope of the Safety Management Systems project substantially different than that originally defined in the approved Safety Management Systems project plan?

213. Have you eliminated all duplicative tasks or manual efforts, where appropriate?

214. Should factors be unpredictable over time?

215. Violation trace: why ?

216. After observing execution of process, is it in compliance with the documented Plan?

217. What strengths do you have?

218. Is there a Steering Committee in place?

219. Does the traceability documentation describe the tool and/or mechanism to be used to capture traceability throughout the life cycle?

220. How relevant is this attribute to this Safety Management Systems project or audit?

221. How can constraints be violated?

2.8 Work Breakdown Structure: Safety Management Systems

222. When does it have to be done?

223. When would you develop a Work Breakdown Structure?

224. Why is it useful?

225. Do you need another level?

226. Where does it take place?

227. Is it still viable?

228. What is the probability that the Safety Management Systems project duration will exceed xx weeks?

229. What has to be done?

230. How big is a work-package?

231. How will you and your Safety Management Systems project team define the Safety Management Systems projects scope and work breakdown structure?

232. How many levels?

233. Is the work breakdown structure (wbs) defined and is the scope of the Safety Management Systems

project clear with assigned deliverable owners?

234. Can you make it?

235. Why would you develop a Work Breakdown Structure?

236. When do you stop?

237. Who has to do it?

2.9 WBS Dictionary: Safety Management Systems

238. Are all authorized tasks assigned to identified organizational elements?

239. Is future work which cannot be planned in detail subdivided to the extent practicable for budgeting and scheduling purposes?

240. Identify potential or actual budget-based and time-based schedule variances?

241. Are overhead costs budgets established on a basis consistent with anticipated direct business base?

242. Evaluate the performance of operating organizations?

243. Do work packages consist of discrete tasks which are adequately described?

244. Software specification, development, integration, and testing, licenses ?

245. Intermediate schedules, as required, which provide a logical sequence from the master schedule to the control account level?

246. Detailed schedules which support control account and work package start and completion dates/events?

247. Wbs elements contractually specified for reporting of status to you (lowest level only)?

248. Do work packages reflect the actual way in which the work will be done and are they meaningful products or management-oriented subdivisions of a higher level element of work?

249. Are overhead cost budgets (or Safety Management Systems projections) established on a facility-wide basis at least annually for the life of the contract?

250. Are time-phased budgets established for planning and control of level of effort activity by category of resource; for example, type of manpower and/or material?

251. The anticipated business volume?

252. What is the goal?

253. Is each control account assigned to a single organizational element directly responsible for the work and identifiable to a single element of the CWBS?

254. What is wrong with this Safety Management Systems project?

255. Does the scheduling system provide for the identification of work progress against technical and other milestones, and also provide for forecasts of completion dates of scheduled work?

256. Are retroactive changes to budgets for completed work specifically prohibited in an established procedure, and is this procedure adhered to?

257. Are all affected work authorizations, budgeting, and scheduling documents amended to properly reflect the effects of authorized changes?

2.10 Schedule Management Plan: Safety Management Systems

258. Timeline and milestones?

259. What tools and techniques will be used to estimate activity durations?

260. Has the Safety Management Systems project scope been baselined?

261. Have all documents been archived in a Safety Management Systems project repository for each release?

262. Are risk oriented checklists used during risk identification?

263. Are the payment terms being followed?

264. Have all unresolved risks been documented?

265. Where is the scheduling tool and who has access to it to view it?

266. Does the Safety Management Systems project have a formal Safety Management Systems project Charter?

267. Are vendor invoices audited for accuracy before payment?

268. Are tasks tracked by hours?

269. What happens if a warning is triggered?

270. Are milestone deliverables effectively tracked and compared to Safety Management Systems project plan?

271. Does the business case include how the Safety Management Systems project aligns with your organizations strategic goals & objectives?

272. Are all activities captured and do they address all approved work scope in the Safety Management Systems project baseline?

273. Do Safety Management Systems project managers participating in the Safety Management Systems project know the Safety Management Systems projects true status first hand?

274. Are the quality tools and methods identified in the Quality Plan appropriate to the Safety Management Systems project?

275. Is the critical path valid?

276. How relevant is this attribute to this Safety Management Systems project or audit?

277. List all schedule constraints here. Must the Safety Management Systems project be complete by a specified date?

2.11 Activity List: Safety Management Systems

278. What went well?

279. How will it be performed?

280. How detailed should a Safety Management Systems project get?

281. How do you determine the late start (LS) for each activity?

282. How can the Safety Management Systems project be displayed graphically to better visualize the activities?

283. How difficult will it be to do specific activities on this Safety Management Systems project?

284. When will the work be performed?

285. What are the critical bottleneck activities?

286. Can you determine the activity that must finish, before this activity can start?

287. What is the probability the Safety Management Systems project can be completed in xx weeks?

288. For other activities, how much delay can be tolerated?

289. What went wrong?

290. In what sequence?

291. What did not go as well?

292. Are the required resources available or need to be acquired?

293. What is the total time required to complete the Safety Management Systems project if no delays occur?

294. How much slack is available in the Safety Management Systems project?

295. Where will it be performed?

2.12 Activity Attributes: Safety Management Systems

296. Why?

297. What is the general pattern here?

298. How much activity detail is required?

299. Were there other ways you could have organized the data to achieve similar results?

300. Do you feel very comfortable with your prediction?

301. What activity do you think you should spend the most time on?

302. Resources to accomplish the work?

303. Activity: what is In the Bag?

304. Where else does it apply?

305. How do you manage time?

306. Does your organization of the data change its meaning?

307. Resource is assigned to?

308. How many resources do you need to complete the work scope within a limit of X number of days?

309. What is missing?

310. Is there anything planned that does not need to be here?

311. Has management defined a definite timeframe for the turnaround or Safety Management Systems project window?

2.13 Milestone List: Safety Management Systems

312. Identify critical paths (one or more) and which activities are on the critical path?

313. Marketing - reach, distribution, awareness?

314. How late can each activity be finished and started?

315. Describe your organizations strengths and core competencies. What factors will make your organization succeed?

316. What date will the task finish?

317. Describe the industry you are in and the market growth opportunities. What is the market for your technology, product or service?

318. Describe the concept of the technology, product or service that will be or has been developed. How will it be used?

319. Calculate how long can activity be delayed?

320. Vital contracts and partners?

321. What would happen if a delivery of material was one week late?

322. What has been done so far?

323. When will the Safety Management Systems project be complete?

324. Sustaining internal capabilities?

325. What is your organizations history in doing similar activities?

326. Loss of key staff?

327. How soon can the activity finish?

328. Reliability of data, plan predictability?

2.14 Network Diagram: Safety Management Systems

329. What job or jobs precede it?

330. Can you calculate the confidence level?

331. What are the Major Administrative Issues?

332. What is the lowest cost to complete this Safety Management Systems project in xx weeks?

333. If x is long, what would be the completion time if you break x into two parallel parts of y weeks and z weeks?

334. Planning: who, how long, what to do?

335. What job or jobs follow it?

336. What activities must occur simultaneously with this activity?

337. Will crashing x weeks return more in benefits than it costs?

338. What activity must be completed immediately before this activity can start?

339. What must be completed before an activity can be started?

340. Where do you schedule uncertainty time?

341. If a current contract exists, can you provide the vendor name, contract start, and contract expiration date?

342. What to do and When?

343. How confident can you be in your milestone dates and the delivery date?

344. Why must you schedule milestones, such as reviews, throughout the Safety Management Systems project?

345. What is the probability of completing the Safety Management Systems project in less that xx days?

346. What controls the start and finish of a job?

347. If the Safety Management Systems project network diagram cannot change and you have extra personnel resources, what is the BEST thing to do?

2.15 Activity Resource Requirements: Safety Management Systems

348. When does monitoring begin?

349. Which logical relationship does the PDM use most often?

350. Why do you do that?

351. What is the Work Plan Standard?

352. Are there unresolved issues that need to be addressed?

353. Do you use tools like decomposition and rolling-wave planning to produce the activity list and other outputs?

354. What are constraints that you might find during the Human Resource Planning process?

355. How do you handle petty cash?

356. Other support in specific areas?

357. How many signatures do you require on a check and does this match what is in your policy and procedures?

358. Organizational Applicability?

359. Time for overtime?

360. Anything else?

2.16 Resource Breakdown Structure: Safety Management Systems

361. What can you do to improve productivity?

362. What is the primary purpose of the human resource plan?

363. Which resource planning tool provides information on resource responsibility and accountability?

364. What is the purpose of assigning and documenting responsibility?

365. Who is allowed to see what data about which resources?

366. What defines a successful Safety Management Systems project?

367. Why time management?

368. The list could probably go on, but, the thing that you would most like to know is, How long & How much?

369. Who will use the system?

370. What are the requirements for resource data?

371. Why do you do it?

372. Who will be used as a Safety Management Systems project team member?

373. Who is allowed to perform which functions?

374. What defines a successful Safety Management Systems project?

375. Changes based on input from stakeholders?

376. Who needs what information?

377. Any changes from stakeholders?

2.17 Activity Duration Estimates: Safety Management Systems

378. Will additional funds be needed for hardware or software?

379. What type of information goes in a quality assurance plan?

380. If Safety Management Systems project time and cost are not as important as the number of resources used each month, which is the BEST thing to do?

381. Write a one to two-page paper describing your dream team for this Safety Management Systems project. What type of people would you want on your team?

382. After how many days will the lease cost be the same as the purchase cost for the equipment?

383. Is a contract developed which obligates the seller and the buyer?

384. Are performance reviews conducted regularly to assess the status of Safety Management Systems projects?

385. How is the Safety Management Systems project doing?

386. What are the main types of contracts if you do decide to outsource?

387. Why is it difficult to use Safety Management Systems project management software well?

388. Is the work performed reviewed against contractual objectives?

389. Safety Management Systems project has three critical paths. Which BEST describes how this affects the Safety Management Systems project?

390. What are two suggestions for ensuring adequate change control on Safety Management Systems projects that involve outside contracts?

391. After changes are approved are Safety Management Systems project documents updated and distributed?

392. Are resource rates available to calculate Safety Management Systems project costs?

393. When would a milestone chart be used instead of a bar char?

394. Do your results resemble a normal distribution?

395. What time management activity should you do NEXT?

396. See what went wrong?

2.18 Duration Estimating Worksheet: Safety Management Systems

397. Will the Safety Management Systems project collaborate with the local community and leverage resources?

398. Science = process: remember the scientific method?

399. When does your organization expect to be able to complete it?

400. Small or large Safety Management Systems project?

401. When, then?

402. What is the total time required to complete the Safety Management Systems project if no delays occur?

403. Define the work as completely as possible. What work will be included in the Safety Management Systems project?

404. Is a construction detail attached (to aid in explanation)?

405. What is cost and Safety Management Systems project cost management?

406. What is your role?

407. What utility impacts are there?

408. Why estimate costs?

409. How should ongoing costs be monitored to try to keep the Safety Management Systems project within budget?

410. Done before proceeding with this activity or what can be done concurrently?

411. What questions do you have?

412. Can the Safety Management Systems project be constructed as planned?

413. Is this operation cost effective?

2.19 Project Schedule: Safety Management Systems

414. Is the Safety Management Systems project schedule available for all Safety Management Systems project team members to review?

415. Safety Management Systems project work estimates Who is managing the work estimate quality of work tasks in the Safety Management Systems project schedule?

416. Did the Safety Management Systems project come in under budget?

417. Did the final product meet or exceed user expectations?

418. How do you use schedules?

419. Is Safety Management Systems project work proceeding in accordance with the original Safety Management Systems project schedule?

420. Are you working on the right risks?

421. Your Safety Management Systems project management plan results in a Safety Management Systems project schedule that is too long. If the Safety Management Systems project network diagram cannot change and you have extra personnel resources, what is the BEST thing to do?

422. What is risk?

423. Have all Safety Management Systems project delays been adequately accounted for, communicated to all stakeholders and adjustments made in overall Safety Management Systems project schedule?

424. Why is software Safety Management Systems project disaster so common?

425. Why do you think schedule issues often cause the most conflicts on Safety Management Systems projects?

426. Verify that the update is accurate. Are all remaining durations correct?

427. How does a Safety Management Systems project get to be a year late ?

428. Why do you need schedules?

429. Did the Safety Management Systems project come in on schedule?

430. Are key risk mitigation strategies added to the Safety Management Systems project schedule?

431. How can you minimize or control changes to Safety Management Systems project schedules?

432. Are quality inspections and review activities listed in the Safety Management Systems project schedule(s)?

2.20 Cost Management Plan: Safety Management Systems

433. Have key stakeholders been identified?

434. Vac -variance at completion, how much over/ under budget do you expect to be?

435. Are decisions captured in a decisions log?

436. Was your organizations estimating methodology being used and followed?

437. Are procurement deliverables arriving on time and to specification?

438. Is the Safety Management Systems project schedule available for all Safety Management Systems project team members to review?

439. Does the business case include how the Safety Management Systems project aligns with your organizations strategic goals & objectives?

440. What does this mean to a cost or scheduler manager?

441. Are post milestone Safety Management Systems project reviews (PMPR) conducted with your organization at least once a year?

442. Has the Safety Management Systems project scope been baselined?

443. Cost tracking and performance analysis – How will cost tracking and performance analysis be accomplished?

444. Is the Safety Management Systems project sponsor clearly communicating the business case or rationale for why this Safety Management Systems project is needed?

445. Is documentation created for communication with the suppliers and Vendors?

446. Mitigation – based on the action, cost and probability of success, will the mitigation be made?

447. Has a capability assessment been conducted?

448. Safety Management Systems project Objectives?

449. Are enough systems & user personnel assigned to the Safety Management Systems project?

450. Is there a formal process for updating the Safety Management Systems project baseline?

2.21 Activity Cost Estimates: Safety Management Systems

451. What were things that you did well, and could improve, and how?

452. In which phase of the acquisition process cycle does source qualifications reside?

453. Review – what are some common errors in activities to avoid?

454. When do you enter into PPM?

455. Certification of actual expenditures?

456. What makes a good expected result statement?

457. Eac -estimate at completion, what is the total job expected to cost?

458. Specific - is the objective clear in terms of what, how, when, and where the situation will be changed?

459. Was it performed on time?

460. Performance bond should always provide what part of the contract value?

461. What areas does the group agree are the biggest success on the Safety Management Systems project?

462. If you are asked to lower your estimate because

the price is too high, what are your options?

463. What is the activity inventory?

464. What is a Safety Management Systems project Management Plan?

465. What is procurement?

466. Does the estimator estimate by task or by person?

467. What makes a good activity description?

468. What procedures are put in place regarding bidding and cost comparisons, if any?

469. Will you need to provide essential services information about activities?

2.22 Cost Estimating Worksheet: Safety Management Systems

470. Does the Safety Management Systems project provide innovative ways for stakeholders to overcome obstacles or deliver better outcomes?

471. Value pocket identification & quantification what are value pockets?

472. Who is best positioned to know and assist in identifying corresponding factors?

473. Can a trend be established from historical performance data on the selected measure and are the criteria for using trend analysis or forecasting methods met?

474. Is it feasible to establish a control group arrangement?

475. Ask: are others positioned to know, are others credible, and will others cooperate?

476. Will the Safety Management Systems project collaborate with the local community and leverage resources?

477. Identify the timeframe necessary to monitor progress and collect data to determine how the selected measure has changed?

478. What is the estimated labor cost today based

upon this information?

479. What additional Safety Management Systems project(s) could be initiated as a result of this Safety Management Systems project?

480. How will the results be shared and to whom?

481. Is the Safety Management Systems project responsive to community need?

482. What can be included?

483. What will others want?

484. What info is needed?

485. What happens to any remaining funds not used?

486. What is the purpose of estimating?

487. What costs are to be estimated?

2.23 Cost Baseline: Safety Management Systems

488. Are procedures defined by which the cost baseline may be changed?

489. What would the life cycle costs be?

490. How will cost estimates be used?

491. Have the actual milestone completion dates been compared to the approved schedule?

492. Are you meeting with your team regularly?

493. Has the actual cost of the Safety Management Systems project (or Safety Management Systems project phase) been tallied and compared to the approved budget?

494. Has operations management formally accepted responsibility for operating and maintaining the product(s) or service(s) delivered by the Safety Management Systems project?

495. Is there anything you need from upper management in order to be successful?

496. When should cost estimates be developed?

497. How do you manage cost?

498. What is the most important thing to do next

to make your Safety Management Systems project successful?

499. Have all approved changes to the cost baseline been identified and impact on the Safety Management Systems project documented?

500. What does a good WBS NOT look like?

501. Is the cr within Safety Management Systems project scope?

502. Definition of done can be traced back to the definitions of what are you providing to the customer in terms of deliverables?

503. Has the Safety Management Systems project documentation been archived or otherwise disposed as described in the Safety Management Systems project communication plan?

504. What do you want to measure ?

505. What deliverables come first?

2.24 Quality Management Plan: Safety Management Systems

506. Who is responsible?

507. You know what your customers expectations are regarding this process?

508. How does your organization determine the requirements and product/service features important to customers?

509. How is staff informed of proper reporting methods?

510. How will you know that a change is actually an improvement?

511. How are corresponding standards measured?

512. How does your organization maintain a safe and healthy work environment?

513. How does your organization ensure the reliability, accuracy, timeliness, security and accessibility of data and information?

514. Results Available?

515. How is the information recorded?

516. Sampling part of task?

517. Were there any deficiencies / issues in prior years self-assessment?

518. How effectively was the Quality Management Plan applied during Safety Management Systems project Execution?

519. What are your organizations current levels and trends for the already stated measures related to financial and marketplace performance?

520. How is equipment calibrated?

521. How does your organization recruit, hire, and retain new employees?

522. Were there any deficiencies / issues identified in the prior years self-assessment?

523. Have adequate resources been provided by management to ensure Safety Management Systems project success?

524. How are calibration records kept?

525. Is the amount of effort justified by the anticipated value of forming a new process?

2.25 Quality Metrics: Safety Management Systems

526. What makes a visualization memorable?

527. How effective are your security tests?

528. What metrics are important and most beneficial to measure?

529. How do you communicate results and findings to upper management?

530. Where is quality now?

531. How do you know if everyone is trying to improve the right things?

532. Product Availability ?

533. Do you know how much profit a 10% decrease in waste would generate?

534. Was material distributed on time?

535. Which are the right metrics to use?

536. Has it met internal or external standards?

537. Are quality metrics defined?

538. Can visual measures help you to filter visualizations of interest?

539. What approved evidence based screening tools can be used?

540. Is quality culture a competitive advantage?

541. What do you measure?

542. How should customers provide input?

543. Have risk areas been identified?

544. How does one achieve stability?

545. Should a modifier be included?

2.26 Process Improvement Plan: Safety Management Systems

546. Why do you want to achieve the goal?

547. Are you making progress on the improvement framework?

548. Who should prepare the process improvement action plan?

549. What personnel are the coaches for your initiative?

550. How do you manage quality?

551. Modeling current processes is great, and will you ever see a return on that investment?

552. Purpose of goal: the motive is determined by asking, why do you want to achieve this goal?

553. Does your process ensure quality?

554. Have the frequency of collection and the points in the process where measurements will be made been determined?

555. Where are you now?

556. To elicit goal statements, do you ask a question such as, What do you want to achieve?

557. What makes people good SPI coaches?

558. What is the test-cycle concept?

559. Are you making progress on the goals?

560. If a process improvement framework is being used, which elements will help the problems and goals listed?

561. Where do you want to be?

562. Has a process guide to collect the data been developed?

563. What actions are needed to address the problems and achieve the goals?

564. Are you meeting the quality standards?

565. Does explicit definition of the measures exist?

2.27 Responsibility Assignment Matrix: Safety Management Systems

566. What is the business need?

567. What simple tool can you use to help identify and prioritize Safety Management Systems project risks that is very low tech and high touch?

568. Budgets assigned to major functional organizations?

569. The staff characteristics – is the group or the person capable to work together as a team?

570. Does each activity-deliverable have exactly one Accountable responsibility, so that accountability is clear and decisions can be made quickly?

571. Are material costs reported within the same period as that in which BCWP is earned for that material?

572. Who is going to do that work?

573. How many people do you need?

574. The total budget for the contract (including estimates for authorized and unpriced work)?

575. Changes in the nature of the overhead requirements?

576. Are meaningful indicators identified for use in measuring the status of cost and schedule performance?

577. Are indirect costs accumulated for comparison with the corresponding budgets?

578. Actual cost of work performed?

579. Is the entire contract planned in time-phased control accounts to the extent practicable?

580. Does the Safety Management Systems project need to be analyzed further to uncover additional responsibilities?

581. Too many rs: with too many people labeled as doing the work, are there too many hands involved?

582. Are records maintained to show how management reserves are used?

583. Are people afraid to let you know when others are under allocated?

2.28 Roles and Responsibilities: Safety Management Systems

584. Concern: where are you limited or have no authority, where you can not influence?

585. Where are you most strong as a supervisor?

586. Are the quality assurance functions and related roles and responsibilities clearly defined?

587. Are governance roles and responsibilities documented?

588. Authority: what areas/Safety Management Systems projects in your work do you have the authority to decide upon and act on the already stated decisions?

589. What should you highlight for improvement?

590. Is feedback clearly communicated and non-judgmental?

591. What should you do now to ensure that you are meeting all expectations of your current position?

592. What specific behaviors did you observe?

593. Have you ever been a part of this team?

594. To decide whether to use a quality measurement, ask how will you know when it is achieved?

595. Do the values and practices inherent in the culture of your organization foster or hinder the process?

596. Once the responsibilities are defined for the Safety Management Systems project, have the deliverables, roles and responsibilities been clearly communicated to every participant?

597. Was the expectation clearly communicated?

598. What areas of supervision are challenging for you?

599. What expectations were met?

600. What areas would you highlight for changes or improvements?

601. What should you do now to prepare yourself for a promotion, increased responsibilities or a different job?

602. Implementation of actions: Who are the responsible units?

2.29 Human Resource Management Plan: Safety Management Systems

603. Did the Safety Management Systems project team have the right skills?

604. Do Safety Management Systems project teams & team members report on status / activities / progress?

605. Are Safety Management Systems project team members committed fulltime?

606. Who is evaluated?

607. Does the schedule include Safety Management Systems project management time and change request analysis time?

608. Are post milestone Safety Management Systems project reviews (PMPR) conducted with your organization at least once a year?

609. Is a pmo (Safety Management Systems project management office) in place and provide oversight to the Safety Management Systems project?

610. Have reserves been created to address risks?

611. Is the current culture aligned with the vision, mission, and values of the department?

612. Is it possible to track all classes of Safety Management Systems project work (e.g. scheduled,

un-scheduled, defect repair, etc.)?

613. Is an industry recognized support tool(s) being used for Safety Management Systems project scheduling & tracking?

614. Is your organization human?

615. Are all payments made according to the contract(s)?

616. Cost / benefit analysis?

617. Do people have the competencies to meet the strategic objectives?

618. Is stakeholder involvement adequate?

619. Has a sponsor been identified?

620. Has your organization readiness assessment been conducted?

621. Based on your Safety Management Systems project communication management plan, what worked well?

622. Is there general agreement & acceptance of the current status and progress of the Safety Management Systems project?

2.30 Communications Management Plan: Safety Management Systems

623. Will messages be directly related to the release strategy or phases of the Safety Management Systems project?

624. Which stakeholders are thought leaders, influences, or early adopters?

625. What to learn?

626. What to know?

627. What data is going to be required?

628. Who needs to know and how much?

629. Do you ask; can you recommend others for you to talk with about this initiative?

630. Who is involved as you identify stakeholders?

631. Who are the members of the governing body?

632. What is the political influence?

633. What communications method?

634. What does the stakeholder need from the team?

635. Who have you worked with in past, similar initiatives?

636. Who to share with?

637. Which stakeholders can influence others?

638. How did the term stakeholder originate?

639. Are others part of the communications management plan?

640. Who is the stakeholder?

2.31 Risk Management Plan: Safety Management Systems

641. How much risk protection can you afford?

642. Are the best people available?

643. Are the participants able to keep up with the workload?

644. What should be done with non-critical risks?

645. How risk averse are you?

646. Minimize cost and financial risk?

647. What things are likely to change?

648. What are the chances the event will occur?

649. Do you manage the process through use of metrics?

650. Are you on schedule?

651. Anticipated volatility of the requirements?

652. Risk documentation: what reporting formats and processes will be used for risk management activities?

653. Are status updates being made on schedule and are the updates clearly described?

654. How would you suggest monitoring for risk transition indicators?

655. How is risk monitoring performed?

656. Market risk -will the new service or product be useful to your organization or marketable to others?

657. Monitoring -what factors can you track that will enable you to determine if the risk is becoming more or less likely?

658. What risks are necessary to achieve success?

659. Have staff received necessary training?

2.32 Risk Register: Safety Management Systems

660. How well are risks controlled?

661. What has changed since the last period?

662. Does the evidence highlight any areas to advance opportunities or foster good relations. If yes what steps will be taken?

663. Recovery actions - planned actions taken once a risk has occurred to allow you to move on. What should you do after?

664. Are there other alternative controls that could be implemented?

665. When will it happen?

666. Severity Prediction?

667. Amongst the action plans and recommendations that you have to introduce are there some that could stop or delay the overall program?

668. What risks might negatively or positively affect achieving the Safety Management Systems project objectives?

669. What can be done about it?

670. Methodology: how will risk management be

performed on this Safety Management Systems project?

671. Are there any gaps in the evidence?

672. Who needs to know about this?

673. How are risks identified?

674. Financial risk -can your organization afford to undertake the Safety Management Systems project?

675. What further options might be available for responding to the risk?

676. Cost/benefit – how much will the proposed mitigations cost and how does this cost compare with the potential cost of the risk event/situation should it occur?

677. How is a Community Risk Register created?

2.33 Probability and Impact Assessment: Safety Management Systems

678. Is the customer willing to commit significant time to the requirements gathering process?

679. Are trained personnel, including supervisors and Safety Management Systems project managers, available to handle such a large Safety Management Systems project?

680. Does the Safety Management Systems project team have experience with the technology to be implemented?

681. How is risk handled within this Safety Management Systems project organization?

682. Are staff committed for the duration of the Safety Management Systems project?

683. Prioritized components/features?

684. How do the products attain the specifications?

685. What significant shift will occur in governmental policies, laws, and regulations pertaining to specific industries?

686. Who are the international/overseas Safety Management Systems project partners (equipment supplier/supplier/consultant/contractor) for this

Safety Management Systems project?

687. Do end-users have realistic expectations?

688. What should be the external organizations responsibility vis-à-vis total stake in the Safety Management Systems project?

689. Which of your Safety Management Systems projects should be selected when compared with other Safety Management Systems projects?

690. How is the Safety Management Systems project going to be managed?

691. Are the software tools integrated with each other?

692. Is the present organizational structure for handling the Safety Management Systems project sufficient?

693. Have decisions that should be left open because of inadequate information on technology been identified and responsibility assigned for reducing the uncertainty?

694. Is the customer willing to establish rapid communication links with the developer?

695. Can this technology be absorbed with current level of expertise available in your organization?

696. Do you have a mechanism for managing change?

2.34 Probability and Impact Matrix: Safety Management Systems

697. Are testing tools available and suitable?

698. What do you expect?

699. What are data sources?

700. What are the current requirements of the customer?

701. Are enough people available?

702. How would you define a risk?

703. What will the damage be?

704. Several experts are offsite, and wish to be included. How can this be done?

705. How realistic is the timing of introduction?

706. Is the customer willing to participate in reviews?

707. Which of your Safety Management Systems projects should be selected when compared with other Safety Management Systems projects?

708. Mandated specific features?

709. Is the process supported by tools?

710. Do the people have the right combinations of skills?

711. What is the level of experience available with your organization?

712. Do you train all developers in the process?

713. What is the political situation at present?

714. Can it be enlarged by drawing people from other areas of your organization?

715. Which of the risk factors can be avoided altogether?

716. Which role do you have in the Safety Management Systems project?

2.35 Risk Data Sheet: Safety Management Systems

717. What actions can be taken to eliminate or remove risk?

718. How can hazards be reduced?

719. How do you handle product safely?

720. Has a sensitivity analysis been carried out?

721. What are the main opportunities available to you that you should grab while you can?

722. During work activities could hazards exist?

723. What was measured?

724. Who has a vested interest in how you perform as your organization (our stakeholders)?

725. What do people affected think about the need for, and practicality of preventive measures?

726. Do effective diagnostic tests exist?

727. What do you know?

728. What will be the consequences if it happens?

729. What are your core values?

730. Whom do you serve (customers)?

731. What were the Causes that contributed?

732. What are the main threats to your existence?

733. What can you do?

734. If it happens, what are the consequences?

735. Potential for recurrence?

736. What is the chance that it will happen?

2.36 Procurement Management Plan: Safety Management Systems

737. What types of contracts will be used?

738. Has a structured approach been used to break work effort into manageable components (WBS)?

739. Do Safety Management Systems project managers participating in the Safety Management Systems project know the Safety Management Systems projects true status first hand?

740. Has Safety Management Systems project success criteria been defined?

741. Has the business need been clearly defined?

742. Is the schedule updated on a periodic basis?

743. Is pert / critical path or equivalent methodology being used?

744. Has a Safety Management Systems project Communications Plan been developed?

745. Is a pmo (Safety Management Systems project management office) in place which provides oversight to the Safety Management Systems project?

746. How long will it take for the purchase cost to be the same as the lease cost?

747. Are enough systems & user personnel assigned to the Safety Management Systems project?

748. Similar Safety Management Systems projects?

749. Are Safety Management Systems project leaders committed to this Safety Management Systems project full time?

750. How will multiple providers be managed?

751. Are the schedule estimates reasonable given the Safety Management Systems project?

752. Does all Safety Management Systems project documentation reside in a common repository for easy access?

753. Does the detailed work plan match the complexity of tasks with the capabilities of personnel?

754. Is a payment system in place with proper reviews and approvals?

755. Are changes in deliverable commitments agreed to by all affected groups & individuals?

2.37 Source Selection Criteria: Safety Management Systems

756. What source selection software is your team using?

757. Does an evaluation need to include the identification of strengths and weaknesses?

758. What is the last item a Safety Management Systems project manager must do to finalize Safety Management Systems project close-out?

759. Do you want to wait until all offerors have been evaluated?

760. Has all proposal data been loaded?

761. How can business terms and conditions be improved to yield more effective price competition?

762. How organization are proposed quotes/prices?

763. Do you have designated specific forms or worksheets?

764. Do you ensure you evaluate what you asked for, not what you want to see or expect to see?

765. What management structure does your organization consider as optimal for performing the contract?

766. How are oral presentations documented?

767. Which contract type places the most risk on the seller?

768. What information may not be provided?

769. Does the evaluation of any change include an impact analysis; how will the change affect the scope, time, cost, and quality of the goods or services being provided?

770. Can you make a cost/technical tradeoff?

771. What documentation is necessary regarding electronic communications?

772. Who must be notified?

773. How should comments received in response to a RFP be handled?

774. What should communications be used to accomplish?

775. How should oral presentations be prepared for?

2.38 Stakeholder Management Plan: Safety Management Systems

776. Are formal code reviews conducted?

777. If a problem has been detected, what tools can be used to determine a root cause?

778. Is there a formal process for updating the Safety Management Systems project baseline?

779. How are you doing/what can be done better?

780. Is the communication plan being followed?

781. How is information analyzed, and what specific pieces of data would be of interest to the Safety Management Systems project manager?

782. Have adequate resources been provided by management to ensure Safety Management Systems project success?

783. Is the process working, and are people executing in compliance of the process?

784. Have the key functions and capabilities been defined and assigned to each release or iteration?

785. Are there any potential occupational health and safety issues due to the proposed purchases?

786. Are issues raised, assessed, actioned, and

resolved in a timely and efficient manner?

787. Were the budget estimates reasonable?

788. What sources of information are reliable?

789. Are Safety Management Systems project contact logs kept up to date?

790. Are the people assigned to the Safety Management Systems project sufficiently qualified?

791. Are there standards for code development?

2.39 Change Management Plan: Safety Management Systems

792. What prerequisite knowledge or training is required?

793. Will a different work structure focus people on what is important?

794. Have the business unit contacts been selected and notified?

795. Which relationships will change?

796. When does it make sense to customize?

797. When to start change management?

798. Who is the audience for change management activities?

799. Who might be able to help you the most?

800. What policies and procedures need to be changed?

801. What prerequisite knowledge do corresponding groups need?

802. What are the essentials of the message?

803. Will you need new processes?

804. Why would a Safety Management Systems project run more smoothly when change management is emphasized from the beginning?

805. How can you best frame the message so that it addresses the audiences interests?

806. What work practices will be affected?

807. Are there any restrictions on who can receive the communications?

808. When should a given message be communicated?

809. What is the reason for the communication?

810. Has an information & communications plan been developed?

811. Is there an adequate supply of people for the new roles?

3.0 Executing Process Group: Safety Management Systems

812. Does software appear easy to learn?

813. Why should Safety Management Systems project managers strive to make jobs look easy?

814. Could a new application negatively affect the current IT infrastructure?

815. What is the product of your Safety Management Systems project?

816. Are decisions made in a timely manner?

817. Who will provide training?

818. What were things that you did very well and want to do the same again on the next Safety Management Systems project?

819. What good practices or successful experiences or transferable examples have been identified?

820. Do the products created live up to the necessary quality?

821. Were sponsors and decision makers available when needed outside regularly scheduled meetings?

822. How well did the chosen processes fit the needs of the Safety Management Systems project?

823. What areas were overlooked on this Safety Management Systems project?

824. When do you share the scorecard with managers?

825. What are the main types of goods and services being outsourced?

826. How do you enter durations, link tasks, and view critical path information?

827. What is the difference between conceptual, application, and evaluative questions?

828. What is in place for ensuring adequate change control on Safety Management Systems projects that involve outside contracts?

829. What are crucial elements of successful Safety Management Systems project plan execution?

830. What is the difference between using brainstorming and the Delphi technique for risk identification?

3.1 Team Member Status Report: Safety Management Systems

831. When a teams productivity and success depend on collaboration and the efficient flow of information, what generally fails them?

832. Does the product, good, or service already exist within your organization?

833. How much risk is involved?

834. Will the staff do training or is that done by a third party?

835. Does every department have to have a Safety Management Systems project Manager on staff?

836. Are your organizations Safety Management Systems projects more successful over time?

837. Are the attitudes of staff regarding Safety Management Systems project work improving?

838. Why is it to be done?

839. Are the products of your organizations Safety Management Systems projects meeting customers objectives?

840. Do you have an Enterprise Safety Management Systems project Management Office (EPMO)?

841. What is to be done?

842. How will resource planning be done?

843. What specific interest groups do you have in place?

844. Does your organization have the means (staff, money, contract, etc.) to produce or to acquire the product, good, or service?

845. The problem with Reward & Recognition Programs is that the truly deserving people all too often get left out. How can you make it practical?

846. How does this product, good, or service meet the needs of the Safety Management Systems project and your organization as a whole?

847. Is there evidence that staff is taking a more professional approach toward management of your organizations Safety Management Systems projects?

848. How it is to be done?

849. How can you make it practical?

3.2 Change Request: Safety Management Systems

850. Who is communicating the change?

851. Who is included in the change control team?

852. Have all related configuration items been properly updated?

853. Are change requests logged and managed?

854. Are there requirements attributes that can discriminate between high and low reliability?

855. What can be filed?

856. Who is responsible to authorize changes?

857. Will all change requests and current status be logged?

858. What are the requirements for urgent changes?

859. Can static requirements change attributes like the size of the change be used to predict reliability in execution?

860. Who is responsible for the implementation and monitoring of all measures?

861. What are the basic mechanics of the Change Advisory Board (CAB)?

862. Who can suggest changes?

863. Who will perform the change?

864. How to get changes (code) out in a timely manner?

865. Where do changes come from?

866. Are there requirements attributes that are strongly related to the occurrence of defects and failures?

867. Will there be a change request form in use?

868. What has an inspector to inspect and to check?

869. Is it feasible to use requirements attributes as predictors of reliability?

3.3 Change Log: Safety Management Systems

870. Is this a mandatory replacement?

871. Do the described changes impact on the integrity or security of the system?

872. Is the change request within Safety Management Systems project scope?

873. When was the request submitted?

874. Who initiated the change request?

875. Will the Safety Management Systems project fail if the change request is not executed?

876. Is the change backward compatible without limitations?

877. When was the request approved?

878. How does this relate to the standards developed for specific business processes?

879. Is the submitted change a new change or a modification of a previously approved change?

880. Should a more thorough impact analysis be conducted?

881. Does the suggested change request seem to

represent a necessary enhancement to the product?

882. How does this change affect scope?

883. How does this change affect the timeline of the schedule?

884. Is the change request open, closed or pending?

885. Is the requested change request a result of changes in other Safety Management Systems project(s)?

886. Does the suggested change request represent a desired enhancement to the products functionality?

3.4 Decision Log: Safety Management Systems

887. Behaviors; what are guidelines that the team has identified that will assist them with getting the most out of team meetings?

888. It becomes critical to track and periodically revisit both operational effectiveness; Are you noticing all that you need to, and are you interpreting what you see effectively?

889. What was the rationale for the decision?

890. With whom was the decision shared or considered?

891. Is everything working as expected?

892. How does the use a Decision Support System influence the strategies/tactics or costs?

893. What is the average size of your matters in an applicable measurement?

894. How do you know when you are achieving it?

895. What is your overall strategy for quality control / quality assurance procedures?

896. Who will be given a copy of this document and where will it be kept?

897. How effective is maintaining the log at facilitating organizational learning?

898. How do you define success?

899. What makes you different or better than others companies selling the same thing?

900. Which variables make a critical difference?

901. At what point in time does loss become unacceptable?

902. Do strategies and tactics aimed at less than full control reduce the costs of management or simply shift the cost burden?

903. What is the line where eDiscovery ends and document review begins?

904. How does provision of information, both in terms of content and presentation, influence acceptance of alternative strategies?

905. Adversarial environment. is your opponent open to a non-traditional workflow, or will it likely challenge anything you do?

906. What are the cost implications?

3.5 Quality Audit: Safety Management Systems

907. What are you trying to accomplish with this audit?

908. How does your organization know that its research programs are appropriately effective and constructive?

909. What does the organizarion look for in a Quality audit?

910. How does your organization know that the system for managing its facilities is appropriately effective and constructive?

911. Does everyone know what they are supposed to be doing, how and why?

912. How does your organization know that its planning processes are appropriately effective and constructive?

913. How do staff know if they are doing a good job?

914. How does your organization know that its Governance system is appropriately effective and constructive?

915. How does your organization know that its staff are presenting original work, and properly acknowledging the work of others?

916. How does your organization know that its system for ensuring a positive organizational climate is appropriately effective and constructive?

917. Does the suppliers quality system have a written procedure for corrective action when a defect occurs?

918. Has a written procedure been established to identify devices during all stages of receipt, reconditioning, distribution and installation so that mix-ups are prevented?

919. Are storage areas and reconditioning operations designed to prevent mix-ups and assure orderly handling of both the distressed and reconditioned devices?

920. How does your organization know that the quality of its supervisors is appropriately effective and constructive?

921. What does an analysis of your organizations staff profile suggest in terms of its planning, and how is this being addressed?

922. Is there any content that may be legally actionable?

923. How does the organization know that its industry and community engagement planning and management systems are appropriately effective and constructive in enabling relationships with key stakeholder groups?

924. How is the Strategic Plan (and other plans)

reviewed and revised?

925. What are you trying to do?

926. How does your organization know that the range and quality of its social and recreational services and facilities are appropriately effective and constructive in meeting the needs of staff?

3.6 Team Directory: Safety Management Systems

927. Who will write the meeting minutes and distribute?

928. Process decisions: how well was task order work performed?

929. Who will report Safety Management Systems project status to all stakeholders?

930. Process decisions: which organizational elements and which individuals will be assigned management functions?

931. Who will be the stakeholders on your next Safety Management Systems project?

932. Who are your stakeholders (customers, sponsors, end users, team members)?

933. Decisions: what could be done better to improve the quality of the constructed product?

934. Contract requirements complied with?

935. Do purchase specifications and configurations match requirements?

936. Where should the information be distributed?

937. Who will talk to the customer?

938. Is construction on schedule?

939. Why is the work necessary?

940. Who should receive information (all stakeholders)?

941. How will the team handle changes?

942. Does a Safety Management Systems project team directory list all resources assigned to the Safety Management Systems project?

943. How and in what format should information be presented?

944. Days from the time the issue is identified?

945. What are you going to deliver or accomplish?

3.7 Team Operating Agreement: Safety Management Systems

946. Are there differences in access to communication and collaboration technology based on team member location?

947. Do you determine the meeting length and time of day?

948. Do you record meetings for the already stated unable to attend?

949. Are there more than two native languages represented by your team?

950. Do you post meeting notes and the recording (if used) and notify participants?

951. Do team members reside in more than two countries?

952. To whom do you deliver your services?

953. Did you determine the technology methods that best match the messages to be communicated?

954. Did you recap the meeting purpose, time, and expectations?

955. What is the anticipated procedure (recruitment, solicitation of volunteers, or assignment) for selecting team members?

956. How will you divide work equitably?

957. Has the appropriate access to relevant data and analysis capability been granted?

958. Did you draft the meeting agenda?

959. Conflict resolution: how will disputes and other conflicts be mediated or resolved?

960. Do you brief absent members after they view meeting notes or listen to a recording?

961. What is a Virtual Team?

962. Must your team members rely on the expertise of other members to complete tasks?

963. Do you prevent individuals from dominating the meeting?

964. How does teaming fit in with overall organizational goals and meet organizational needs?

3.8 Team Performance Assessment: Safety Management Systems

965. To what degree will team members, individually and collectively, commit time to help themselves and others learn and develop skills?

966. To what degree can the team measure progress against specific goals?

967. To what degree is the team cognizant of small wins to be celebrated along the way?

968. To what degree does the teams purpose constitute a broader, deeper aspiration than just accomplishing short-term goals?

969. To what degree is there a sense that only the team can succeed?

970. To what degree are the goals ambitious?

971. Where to from here?

972. Which situations call for a more extreme type of adaptiveness in which team members actually re-define roles?

973. To what degree will the team adopt a concrete, clearly understood, and agreed-upon approach that will result in achievement of the teams goals?

974. To what degree do team members feel that the

purpose of the team is important, if not exciting?

975. What do you think is the most constructive thing that could be done now to resolve considerations and disputes about method variance?

976. What makes opportunities more or less obvious?

977. If you have criticized someones work for method variance in your role as reviewer, what was the circumstance?

978. When a reviewer complains about method variance, what is the essence of the complaint?

979. Social categorization and intergroup behaviour: Does minimal intergroup discrimination make social identity more positive?

980. If you are worried about method variance before you collect data, what sort of design elements might you include to reduce or eliminate the threat of method variance?

981. Delaying market entry: how long is too long?

982. To what degree are the relative importance and priority of the goals clear to all team members?

983. To what degree do members articulate the goals beyond the team membership?

3.9 Team Member Performance Assessment: Safety Management Systems

984. To what degree are sub-teams possible or necessary?

985. New skills/knowledge gained this year?

986. What changes do you need to make to align practices with beliefs?

987. Who should attend?

988. For what period of time is a member rated?

989. What are the staffs preferences for training on technology-based platforms?

990. What tools are available to determine whether all contract functional and compliance areas of performance objectives, measures, and incentives have been met?

991. What happens if a team member receives a Rating of Unsatisfactory?

992. In what areas would you like to concentrate your knowledge and resources?

993. Are any governance changes sufficient to impact achievement?

994. What instructional strategies were developed/incorporated (e.g., direct instruction, indirect instruction, experiential learning, independent study, interactive instruction)?

995. How effective is training that is delivered through technology-based platforms?

996. To what degree do team members understand one anothers roles and skills?

997. What is the target group for instruction (e.g., individual and collective or small team instruction)?

998. What were the challenges that resulted for training and assessment?

999. Verify business objectives. Are they appropriate, and well-articulated?

1000. What are best practices for delivering and developing training evaluations to maximize the benefits of leveraging emerging technologies?

1001. Who they are?

1002. To what degree does the teams purpose contain themes that are particularly meaningful and memorable?

1003. To what extent are systems and applications (e.g., game engine, mobile device platform) utilized?

3.10 Issue Log: Safety Management Systems

1004. Is access to the Issue Log controlled?

1005. Can an impact cause deviation beyond team, stage or Safety Management Systems project tolerances?

1006. In classifying stakeholders, which approach to do so are you using?

1007. Are the stakeholders getting the information they need, are they consulted, are concerns addressed?

1008. How much time does it take to do it?

1009. Are stakeholder roles recognized by your organization?

1010. What is the stakeholders political influence?

1011. What is a Stakeholder?

1012. How do you manage communications?

1013. Who is the issue assigned to?

1014. Who were proponents/opponents?

1015. What is a change?

1016. Why do you manage communications?

1017. Who do you turn to if you have questions?

1018. Do you have members of your team responsible for certain stakeholders?

1019. What is the status of the issue?

1020. Do you often overlook a key stakeholder or stakeholder group?

1021. What would have to change?

4.0 Monitoring and Controlling Process Group: Safety Management Systems

1022. What departments are involved in its daily operation?

1023. How many potential communications channels exist on the Safety Management Systems project?

1024. Is it what was agreed upon?

1025. Based on your Safety Management Systems project communication management plan, what worked well?

1026. Feasibility: how much money, time, and effort can you put into this?

1027. Is there undesirable impact on staff or resources?

1028. Who needs to be involved in the planning?

1029. Just how important is your work to the overall success of the Safety Management Systems project?

1030. Is there sufficient funding available for this?

1031. What kinds of things in particular are you looking for data on?

1032. When will the Safety Management Systems

project be done?

1033. Did you implement the program as designed?

1034. Where is the Risk in the Safety Management Systems project?

1035. What is the timeline?

1036. How to ensure validity, quality and consistency?

1037. What are the goals of the program?

1038. What is the expected monetary value of the Safety Management Systems project?

1039. How were collaborations developed, and how are they sustained?

1040. What are the deliverables?

4.1 Project Performance Report: Safety Management Systems

1041. To what degree do the goals specify concrete team work products?

1042. To what degree do team members articulate the teams work approach?

1043. To what degree can the team ensure that all members are individually and jointly accountable for the teams purpose, goals, approach, and work-products?

1044. To what degree does the information network provide individuals with the information they require?

1045. To what degree is there centralized control of information sharing?

1046. What is the PRS?

1047. To what degree does the informal organization make use of individual resources and meet individual needs?

1048. To what degree do all members feel responsible for all agreed-upon measures?

1049. To what degree does the funding match the requirement?

1050. To what degree will the approach capitalize

on and enhance the skills of all team members in a manner that takes into consideration other demands on members of the team?

1051. Next Steps?

1052. How is the data used?

1053. To what degree does the teams work approach provide opportunity for members to engage in results-based evaluation?

1054. To what degree does the teams work approach provide opportunity for members to engage in fact-based problem solving?

1055. To what degree can team members meet frequently enough to accomplish the teams ends?

4.2 Variance Analysis: Safety Management Systems

1056. Can the contractor substantiate work package and planning package budgets?

1057. Does the contractors system include procedures for measuring the performance of critical subcontractors?

1058. Contract line items and end items?

1059. Is cost and schedule performance measurement done in a consistent, systematic manner?

1060. What is the expected future profitability of each customer?

1061. What business event causes fluctuations?

1062. Did a new competitor enter the market?

1063. Are the bases and rates for allocating costs from each indirect pool consistently applied?

1064. Are the requirements for all items of overhead established by rational, traceable processes?

1065. Did an existing competitor change strategy?

1066. What types of services and expense are shared between business segments?

1067. Are all elements of indirect expense identified to overhead cost budgets of Safety Management Systems projections?

1068. Are there quarterly budgets with quarterly performance comparisons?

1069. What are the direct labor dollars and/or hours?

1070. What is your organizations rationale for sharing expenses and services between business segments?

1071. Are control accounts opened and closed based on the start and completion of work contained therein?

1072. Who are responsible for overhead performance control of related costs?

1073. Are there changes in the direct base to which overhead costs are allocated?

4.3 Earned Value Status: Safety Management Systems

1074. Verification is a process of ensuring that the developed system satisfies the stakeholders agreements and specifications; Are you building the product right? What do you verify?

1075. Where is evidence-based earned value in your organization reported?

1076. When is it going to finish?

1077. What is the unit of forecast value?

1078. If earned value management (EVM) is so good in determining the true status of a Safety Management Systems project and Safety Management Systems project its completion, why is it that hardly any one uses it in information systems related Safety Management Systems projects?

1079. Where are your problem areas?

1080. How much is it going to cost by the finish?

1081. Earned value can be used in almost any Safety Management Systems project situation and in almost any Safety Management Systems project environment. it may be used on large Safety Management Systems projects, medium sized Safety Management Systems projects, tiny Safety Management Systems projects (in cut-down form), complex and simple Safety Management Systems projects and in any market sector. some people, of course, know all about earned value, they have used it for years - but perhaps not as effectively as they could have?

1082. How does this compare with other Safety Management Systems projects?

1083. Validation is a process of ensuring that the developed system will actually achieve the stakeholders desired outcomes; Are you building the right product? What do you validate?

1084. Are you hitting your Safety Management Systems projects targets?

4.4 Risk Audit: Safety Management Systems

1085. Has risk management been considered when planning an event?

1086. Is the auditor truly independent?

1087. Are all managers or operators of the facility or equipment competent or qualified?

1088. Does your auditor understand your business?

1089. What are the outcomes you are looking for?

1090. Are corresponding safety and risk management policies posted for all to see?

1091. Are tool mentors available?

1092. Do industry specialists and business risk auditors enhance audit reporting accuracy?

1093. What can be measured?

1094. Do you conduct risk assessments on all programs, activities and events?

1095. Should additional substantive testing be conducted because of the risk audit results?

1096. Are team members trained in the use of the tools?

1097. How do you manage risk?

1098. Is the number of people on the Safety Management Systems project team adequate to do the job?

1099. What expertise does the Board have on quality, outcomes, and errors?

1100. Are auditors able to effectively apply more soft evidence found in the risk-assessment process with the results of more tangible audit evidence found through more substantive testing?

1101. Are all participants informed of safety issues?

1102. Do all coaches/instructors/leaders have appropriate and current accreditation?

4.5 Contractor Status Report: Safety Management Systems

1103. What is the average response time for answering a support call?

1104. Who can list a Safety Management Systems project as organization experience, your organization or a previous employee of your organization?

1105. What was the actual budget or estimated cost for your organizations services?

1106. What was the budget or estimated cost for your organizations services?

1107. How long have you been using the services?

1108. What process manages the contracts?

1109. What are the minimum and optimal bandwidth requirements for the proposed solution?

1110. How is risk transferred?

1111. Are there contractual transfer concerns?

1112. Describe how often regular updates are made to the proposed solution. Are corresponding regular updates included in the standard maintenance plan?

1113. What was the final actual cost?

1114. If applicable; describe your standard schedule for new software version releases. Are new software version releases included in the standard maintenance plan?

1115. How does the proposed individual meet each requirement?

1116. What was the overall budget or estimated cost?

4.6 Formal Acceptance: Safety Management Systems

1117. What are the requirements against which to test, Who will execute?

1118. What features, practices, and processes proved to be strengths or weaknesses?

1119. Do you buy pre-configured systems or build your own configuration?

1120. What lessons were learned about your Safety Management Systems project management methodology?

1121. How well did the team follow the methodology?

1122. Who supplies data?

1123. Does it do what Safety Management Systems project team said it would?

1124. Do you perform formal acceptance or burn-in tests?

1125. Did the Safety Management Systems project achieve its MOV?

1126. Was the client satisfied with the Safety Management Systems project results?

1127. Was the Safety Management Systems project

goal achieved?

1128. Do you buy-in installation services?

1129. What was done right?

1130. Is formal acceptance of the Safety Management Systems project product documented and distributed?

1131. Was the Safety Management Systems project work done on time, within budget, and according to specification?

1132. Did the Safety Management Systems project manager and team act in a professional and ethical manner?

1133. How does your team plan to obtain formal acceptance on your Safety Management Systems project?

1134. Was the sponsor/customer satisfied?

1135. What function(s) does it fill or meet?

1136. Was the Safety Management Systems project managed well?

5.0 Closing Process Group: Safety Management Systems

1137. How well defined and documented were the Safety Management Systems project management processes you chose to use?

1138. What is an Encumbrance?

1139. Did the Safety Management Systems project team have the right skills?

1140. Is this a follow-on to a previous Safety Management Systems project?

1141. Is this a follow-on to a previous Safety Management Systems project?

1142. How critical is the Safety Management Systems project success to the success of your organization?

1143. Can the lesson learned be replicated?

1144. What areas were overlooked on this Safety Management Systems project?

1145. What were things that you need to improve?

1146. What is the amount of funding and what Safety Management Systems project phases are funded?

1147. Did the delivered product meet the specified requirements and goals of the Safety Management

Systems project?

1148. What is the Safety Management Systems project name and date of completion?

1149. Just how important is your work to the overall success of the Safety Management Systems project?

1150. Were decisions made in a timely manner?

1151. How well did the team follow the chosen processes?

1152. Does the close educate others to improve performance?

1153. If a risk event occurs, what will you do?

1154. Were risks identified and mitigated?

5.1 Procurement Audit: Safety Management Systems

1155. Did your organization calculate the contract value accurately?

1156. Has guidelines been set up for how the procurement function/unit should carry out its procurements?

1157. If information was withheld, was there reasonable justification for this decision?

1158. Has your organization procedures in place to monitor the input of experts employed to assist the procurement function?

1159. Relevance of the contract to the Internal Market?

1160. Where funding is being arranged by borrowings, do corresponding have the necessary approval and legal authority?

1161. When performance conditions were detailed in the tender documentation, did the contracting authority verify if the tenders received met the already stated requirements?

1162. Are the number of checking accounts where cash segregation is not required kept to a reasonable number?

1163. Does the procurement Safety Management Systems project comply with European Communities regulations and rules?

1164. Are contract changes after awarding properly justified and executed?

1165. Are there established procedures for dealing with and documenting non-performance and return of goods?

1166. Is there time waste during tendering?

1167. Are all purchase orders reviewed by someone other than the individual preparing the purchase order (reasonableness of order and vendor selection)?

1168. Was invitation to tender to each specific contract issued after the evaluation of the indicative tenders was completed?

1169. Which are necessary components of a financial audit report under the Single Audit Act?

1170. Were additional works strictly necessary for the completion of performance under the contract?

1171. Are the users needs clearly and invariably defined and has the expected outcome or mission been clearly identified and communicated in measurable terms?

1172. Were results of the award procedures published?

1173. In a competitive dialogue, were solutions

proposed or confidential information given by a candidate not revealed to others without his/her express agreement?

1174. Are all purchase orders accounted for?

5.2 Contract Close-Out: Safety Management Systems

1175. Change in circumstances?

1176. Parties: who is involved?

1177. Have all acceptance criteria been met prior to final payment to contractors?

1178. Change in knowledge?

1179. Have all contract records been included in the Safety Management Systems project archives?

1180. Was the contract complete without requiring numerous changes and revisions?

1181. Parties: Authorized?

1182. Was the contract type appropriate?

1183. Have all contracts been closed?

1184. How/when used ?

1185. How is the contracting office notified of the automatic contract close-out?

1186. Has each contract been audited to verify acceptance and delivery?

1187. Change in attitude or behavior?

1188. Was the contract sufficiently clear so as not to result in numerous disputes and misunderstandings?

1189. What is capture management?

1190. What happens to the recipient of services?

1191. How does it work?

1192. Why Outsource?

1193. Are the signers the authorized officials?

1194. Have all contracts been completed?

5.3 Project or Phase Close-Out: Safety Management Systems

1195. What were the actual outcomes?

1196. What are the mandatory communication needs for each stakeholder?

1197. What could be done to improve the process?

1198. What is the information level of detail required for each stakeholder?

1199. What information did each stakeholder need to contribute to the Safety Management Systems projects success?

1200. Who are the Safety Management Systems project stakeholders and what are roles and involvement?

1201. What were the goals and objectives of the communications strategy for the Safety Management Systems project?

1202. What was expected from each stakeholder?

1203. What process was planned for managing issues/ risks?

1204. What are they?

1205. Is there a clear cause and effect between the

activity and the lesson learned?

1206. Does the lesson educate others to improve performance?

1207. How much influence did the stakeholder have over others?

1208. What are the marketing communication needs for each stakeholder?

1209. What is this stakeholder expecting?

1210. What is in it for you?

1211. What was the preferred delivery mechanism?

1212. How often did each stakeholder need an update?

1213. Planned completion date?

5.4 Lessons Learned: Safety Management Systems

1214. What are the expectations of the individuals?

1215. What is the fiscal dependency?

1216. How timely were Progress Reports provided to the Safety Management Systems project Manager by Team Members?

1217. How spontaneous are the communications?

1218. What were the most significant issues on this Safety Management Systems project?

1219. Did the Safety Management Systems project management methodology work?

1220. Did the team work well together?

1221. What is your organizations performance history?

1222. What is the frequency of communication?

1223. Are new goals needed?

1224. How effectively were issues managed on the Safety Management Systems project?

1225. How was the quality of products/processes assured?

1226. What things mattered the most on this Safety Management Systems project?

1227. Was any formal risk assessment carried out at the start of the Safety Management Systems project, and was this followed up during the Safety Management Systems project?

1228. What did you put in place to ensure success?

1229. Do you have any real problems?

1230. What is the impact of tax policy?

1231. How many interest groups are stakeholders?

1232. What were the challenges and pitfalls?

Index

ability 37, 79
absent 234
absorbed   205
acceptable   54, 88, 94, 143
acceptance   7, 114, 141, 143, 145, 197, 227, 253-254, 260
accepted   112, 140, 151, 184
access 2, 8-10, 23, 65, 135, 144, 158, 211, 233-234, 239
accomplish   8, 81, 106, 112, 133, 162, 213, 228, 232, 244
accordance   176
according   35, 40, 197, 254
account   29, 55, 155-156
accounted   177, 259
accounts   193, 246, 257
accuracy   151, 158, 186, 249
accurate   10, 126, 177
accurately   130, 257
achievable   108
achieve   8, 71, 78-79, 117, 120, 162, 189-191, 201, 248, 253
achieved   18, 78, 82, 112, 194, 254
achieving   202, 226
acquire   221
acquired   161
across 45
action 50, 54, 91, 98-99, 179, 190, 202, 229
actionable   52, 115, 229
actioned   214
actions21, 93, 100, 119, 150, 191, 195, 202, 208
active 137
activities   20, 23-24, 30, 82, 97, 99, 117, 130, 137, 159-160,
164-166, 177, 180-181, 196, 200, 208, 216, 249
activity3-4, 30, 39, 156, 158, 160, 162, 164-166, 168, 172-173, 175,
180-181, 263
actual 39, 54, 143, 155-156, 180, 184, 193, 251, 262
actually   34, 66, 84, 142, 186, 235, 248
addition   114
additional   32, 58, 62, 66, 70, 172, 183, 193, 249, 258
additions   99
address   25, 77, 132, 159, 191, 196
addressed   139, 168, 229, 239
addresses   217

addressing   37, 109
adequate   28, 140, 151, 173, 187, 197, 214, 217, 219, 250
adequately   32, 155, 177
adhered   157
adjust 101
adjusted   95
adopted   138
adopters   198
advance   202
advantage   71, 103, 189
advantages   114
Advisory   222
affect 61-62, 67, 115, 121, 130, 138, 141, 147, 151, 202, 213, 218, 225
affected   135, 157, 208, 211, 217
affecting   12, 19, 69
affects 173
afford 200, 203
affordable   84
afraid 193
against32, 96, 101, 156, 173, 235, 253
agenda   130, 234
agendas   122
aggregate   45
agreed   211, 241
agreement   6, 107, 197, 233, 259
agreements   70, 84, 247
agrees 105
aiming 120
alerts 98
aligned   19, 196
aligns 159, 178
alleged   1
alliance   77
allocate   105
allocated   51, 57, 110, 193, 246
allocating   245
allowed   123, 170-171
allows 10
almost 247
already   124, 187, 194, 220, 233, 257
Although   130
altogether   207

always 10, 180
ambitious   235
amended   157
Amongst   202
amount   21, 187, 255
amplify68, 110
analysis   3, 6, 10-11, 58, 60, 64, 67, 69-70, 82, 135, 140, 179,
182, 196-197, 208, 213, 224, 229, 234, 245
analyze   2, 58, 63, 66
analyzed   98, 130, 193, 214
analyzes   139
annually   156
another   153
anothers   238
answer 11-12, 16, 28, 44, 58, 74, 90, 103
answered   27, 43, 57, 73, 89, 102, 127
answering   11, 251
anyone   31, 113, 122
anything   163, 169, 184, 227
appear   1, 218
applicable   11, 92, 226, 252
applied   88, 95, 187, 245
appointed   29, 39
approach   84, 89, 114, 119, 151, 210, 221, 235, 239, 243-244
approaches   86
approval   39, 257
approvals   142, 211
approved   42, 65, 130, 140, 147, 150, 152, 159, 173, 184-185,
189, 224
approving   147
Architects   8
archived   158, 185
archives   260
around113, 119
arranged   257
arriving178
articulate   236, 243
asking 1, 8, 190
aspects   135
aspiration   235
assess 25, 36, 80, 95, 108, 172
assessed   88, 214
assessing   91

Assessment   5-6, 9-10, 22, 179, 197, 204, 235, 237-238, 265
assign 18
assigned   32, 139, 149, 154-156, 162, 179, 192, 205, 211,
214-215, 231-232, 239
assigning   170
Assignment   5, 192, 233
assist   9, 72, 75, 90, 182, 226, 257
assistant   8
associated   129
Assumption   3, 151
assurance   23, 172, 194, 226
assure 229
assured   264
attached   174
attain 204
attainable   32
attempted   31
attempting   94
attend 16, 233, 237
attendance   29
attendant   79
attended   29
attention   12, 115
attitude   260
attitudes   220
attribute   142, 152, 159
attributes   3, 123, 162, 222-223
audience   216
audiences   217
audited   158, 260
auditing   18, 97, 125
auditor 249
auditors   249-250
author 1
authority   65, 194, 257
authorize   222
authorized   141, 155, 157, 192, 260-261
automatic   260
available   20, 23, 32, 38, 46, 59, 71, 87, 90, 118, 161, 173,
176, 178, 186, 200, 203-208, 218, 237, 241, 249
Average   12, 27, 43, 57, 73, 89, 102, 127, 226, 251
averse 200
avoided   207

awarding   258
awareness   164
background   10
backward   224
balanced   80
bandwidth   251
baseline   4, 140, 143, 159, 179, 184-185, 214
baselined   158, 178
baselines   29-30
basics 122
because   180, 205, 249
become   69, 109, 115, 124, 147, 227
becomes   226
becoming   201
before 10, 31, 94, 141, 158, 160, 166, 175, 236
beginning   2, 15, 27, 43, 57, 73, 89, 102, 127, 217
begins 227
behavior   260
behaviors   20, 194, 226
behaviour   236
belief   11, 16, 28, 44, 58, 74, 90, 103, 123
beliefs 237
believable   108
believe105, 123
beneficial   188
benefit 1, 21-22, 24, 47, 93, 197, 203
benefits   24, 45, 47, 56, 70, 103, 112, 114, 120-121, 124, 132, 166, 238
better 8, 35, 51, 78, 160, 182, 214, 227, 231
between   59, 147, 219, 222, 245-246, 262
beyond   236, 239
bidding   181
biggest   45, 80, 180
blinding   65
borrowings   257
bother 49
bottleneck   160
boundaries   33
bounds   33
Breakdown   3-4, 153-154, 170
briefed39
brings 38
broader   235

broken 71
budget   92, 94, 118, 139, 141, 175-176, 178, 184, 192, 215,
251-252, 254
budgeted   54
budgeting   155, 157
budgets   20, 105, 155-157, 192-193, 245-246
building   21, 99, 132, 247-248
burden 227
burn-in 253
business   1, 8, 10, 24-25, 36, 47, 52, 66, 69, 72, 82, 86, 96,
104, 107, 109-110, 112, 115, 120, 122, 124, 126, 129, 146, 150,
155-156, 159, 178-179, 192, 210, 212, 216, 224, 238, 245-246, 249
buy-in   105, 254
calculate   164, 166, 173, 257
calibrated   187
candidate   259
cannot 155, 167, 176
capability   25, 133, 179, 234
capable   8, 34, 192
capacities   123, 138
capacity   21, 25, 83, 133
capital 104
capitalize   67, 243
capture   52, 97, 152, 261
captured   56, 68, 77, 126, 141, 159, 178
career 147
careers   126
carried 69, 208, 265
category   36, 156
caused   1, 56
causes 47, 50, 54, 58-59, 66, 93, 139-140, 209, 245
causing   19
celebrate   77
celebrated   235
center 55, 139
centrally   80
certain 240
challenge   8, 227
challenges   123, 129, 238, 265
chance   209
chances   200

change   5-6, 16, 42, 52-53, 67, 69-70, 72, 80-81, 84, 100,
123, 132, 134, 139-140, 143, 149, 162, 167, 173, 176, 186, 196,
200, 205, 213, 216-217, 219, 222-225, 239-240, 245, 260
changed   17, 42, 100, 105, 146, 180, 182, 184, 202, 216
changes   21, 30, 35, 40, 47, 65, 76, 79, 94, 99, 114-115, 125-
126, 130, 139, 141, 145, 157, 171, 173, 177, 185, 192, 195, 211,
222-225, 232, 237, 246, 258, 260
changing   101, 119
channels   241
charged   46
Charter   2, 36-37, 83, 132-133, 158
charts 73
cheaper   51
checked   68, 91, 93, 95, 146
checking   257
checklists   9, 158
choice 36, 119
choose   11, 125
chosen 138, 218, 256
circumvent   23
claimed   1
classes 196
clearly 11, 16, 27-28, 37, 40, 42, 44, 58, 61, 74, 90, 103, 142, 149,
179, 194-195, 200, 210, 235, 258
client   48, 118, 253
clients 18, 36
climate   229
closed 101, 225, 246, 260
closely 10
Close-Out   7, 212, 260, 262
closest 118
Closing 7, 70, 255
coaches   31, 190-191, 250
cognizant   235
colleague   116
colleagues   108
collect 61, 91, 182, 191, 236
collected   35, 41, 58, 61-62, 65, 68, 73
collection   69, 190
collective   238
combine   86
command   97
comments   213

commit 204, 235
commitment 100, 113, 136
committed 66, 196, 204, 211
Committee 152
common 150, 177, 180, 211
community 174, 182-183, 203, 229
companies 1, 93, 227
company 8, 51, 71, 110, 115-116, 119, 122, 126
comparable 140
compare 62, 85, 118, 203, 248
compared 110, 159, 184, 205-206
comparing 140
comparison 11, 193
compatible 224
compelling 29
competent 249
competing 51
competitor 245
complains 236
complaint 236
complete 1, 9, 11, 20, 30, 36, 38, 140, 159, 161-162, 165-166, 174, 234, 260
completed 12, 37-38, 41, 43, 141, 157, 160, 166, 258, 261
completely 174
completing 118, 167
completion 30, 34, 155-156, 166, 178, 180, 184, 246-247, 256, 258, 263
complex 8, 121, 248
complexity 21, 50, 67, 211
compliance 26, 52, 84, 132, 151-152, 214, 237
complied 231
comply 258
components 204, 210, 258
compute 12
concept 81, 150, 164, 191
concepts 107
conceptual 219
concern 49, 77, 194
concerned 26
concerns 18-19, 118, 239, 251
concrete 75, 235, 243
condition 91, 138
conditions 95, 114, 135, 212, 257

conduct 249
conducted 141, 172, 178-179, 196-197, 214, 224, 249
confidence 166
confident 167
confirm 11
Conflict 234
conflicts 177, 234
conjure 146
connecting 104
consider 19, 23-24, 133, 212
considered 23-24, 50, 226, 249
considers 71
consist 155
consistent 38, 46, 94, 151, 155, 245
constitute 235
Constraint 3, 151
consultant 8, 204
consulted 106, 239
consulting 51
consumers 105
contact 8, 215
contacts 124, 216
contain 25, 70, 101, 140, 238
contained 1, 246
contains 9
content 42, 140, 151, 227, 229
contents 1-2, 9
context 41-43
continual 92, 101
Continuity 135
continuous 60, 88
contract 7, 156, 167, 172, 180, 192-193, 197, 212-213, 221, 231, 237, 245, 257-258, 260-261
Contractor 7, 204, 245, 251
contracts 39, 70, 164, 172-173, 210, 219, 251, 260-261
contribute 145, 262
control 2, 39, 55, 73, 90, 94-100, 135, 140, 143, 149, 155-156, 173, 177, 182, 193, 219, 222, 226-227, 243, 246
controlled 70, 202, 239
controls 25, 59, 72, 78, 88-89, 95-96, 100, 167, 202
convention 104
convey 1
cooperate 182

Copyright   1
correct44, 90, 139, 177
corrective   93, 229
correspond   9-10
costing53
counting   113, 143
countries   233
counts 113
course 42, 52, 248
covered   130
covering   9, 96
coworker   118
crashing   166
craziest   123
create 24, 105, 110, 114
created   60, 68, 100, 134, 138-139, 179, 196, 203, 218
creating   8, 45, 137
creative   25
creativity   86
credible   182
criteria 2, 5, 9-10, 32, 36, 75, 78, 80, 91, 108, 121, 128, 141, 145,
147, 182, 210, 212, 260
CRITERION   2, 16, 28, 44, 58, 74, 90, 103
critical 29, 35, 42, 68, 74, 100, 125, 130, 159-160, 164, 173, 210,
219, 226-227, 245, 255
criticism   60
criticized   236
crucial 59, 135, 219
crystal 11
culture 35, 69, 189, 195-196
current38, 44, 59, 61-62, 64, 84, 92, 107, 112, 120, 123-124, 151-
152, 167, 187, 190, 194, 196-197, 205-206, 218, 222, 250
currently   35, 113
custom18
customer   23, 32, 35-36, 40-42, 78, 91, 97, 110, 116-117, 127,
132, 149-150, 185, 204-206, 231, 245, 254
customers   1, 25, 29, 41, 48, 52, 54, 61-62, 93, 105, 107, 109,
111, 113, 115, 119, 121, 123, 150, 152, 186, 189, 209, 220, 231
customize   216
cut-down   247
cycles 132
damage   1, 206
Dashboard   9

dashboards 99
day-to-day 92, 104
deadlines 23, 120
dealing 258
deceitful 118
decide 172, 194
decided 125
deciding 121
decision 6, 45, 62, 74-75, 80-81, 84, 130, 218, 226, 257
decisions 75-76, 78-79, 83, 87-88, 90, 94, 101, 132, 178, 192, 194, 205, 218, 231, 256
decrease 188
dedicated 8
deeper 11, 235
defect 197, 229
defects 223
define 2, 28, 31, 35, 71-72, 77, 150, 153, 174, 206, 227
defined 11, 16, 18, 25, 28-30, 33, 37, 39-42, 44, 58, 70-71, 74, 90, 103, 142, 149-153, 163, 184, 188, 194-195, 210, 214, 255, 258
defines 19, 32, 41, 170-171
defining 8, 117
definite 101, 163
definition 19, 27, 32-34, 185, 191
degree 235-238, 243-244
delayed 164
Delaying 50, 236
delays 52, 161, 174, 177
delegated 34
deletions 99
deliver 25, 29, 78, 107, 112, 182, 232-233
delivered 56, 121, 142, 144, 184, 238, 255
delivering 238
delivery 17, 47, 107, 114, 164, 167, 260, 263
Delphi 219
demand 112
demands 244
department 8, 110, 196, 220
depend 220
dependency 264
dependent 107
depends 115
deploy 98, 111

deployed   98
deploying   51
derive 91
Describe   24, 147, 152, 164, 251-252
described   1, 155, 185, 200, 224
describes   173
describing   41, 172
deserving   221
design 1, 10, 63, 77, 80, 97, 119, 151-152, 236
designated   212
designed   8, 10, 58, 88, 229, 242
designing   8
desired20, 32, 62, 81, 225, 248
detail   80, 150, 155, 162, 174, 262
detailed   67-68, 141, 144, 155, 160, 211, 257
detect 95
detected   214
determine   10, 120-121, 160, 182, 186, 201, 214, 233, 237
determined   60, 121, 190
determines   136
develop   74, 80, 82-83, 153-154, 235
developed   10, 36-37, 43, 47, 75, 83, 140, 143, 164, 172, 184,
191, 210, 217, 224, 238, 242, 247-248
developer   205
developers   207
developing   63, 81, 238
deviation   239
device 238
devices   229
diagnostic   208
diagram   4, 45, 47, 66, 166-167, 176
diagrams   49
dialogue   258
Dictionary   3, 155
difference   130, 219, 227
different   8, 26, 29, 34, 40, 66, 72, 121, 138, 152, 195, 216,
227
difficult59, 160, 173
dimensions   17
direct   155, 238, 246
direction   42, 51, 139-140
directly1, 61-62, 130, 156, 198
Directory   6, 231-232

Disagree   11, 16, 28, 44, 58, 74, 90, 103
disaster   50, 177
disclosure   93
discrete   155
discussion   109
displayed   35, 63, 160
disposed   185
disputes   234, 236, 261
disqualify   66
disruptive   72
distressed   229
distribute   231
divide 234
Divided   27, 34, 43, 57, 73, 89, 102, 127
division 139
document   10, 30, 130, 132, 140, 145, 151, 226-227
documented 35, 78, 94, 98, 129, 149, 151-152, 158, 185, 194,
213, 254-255
documents   8, 151, 157-158, 173
dollars 246
domains   81
dominating   234
dormant   124
drawing   207
Driver   70
drivers 49, 66, 69
drives   49
driving 105
Duration   4, 138, 153, 172, 174, 204
durations   39, 158, 177, 219
during 42, 82, 129, 158, 168, 187, 208, 229, 258, 265
dynamics   34
earlier 123
earned   6, 192, 247-248
economical   106
economy   79
eDiscovery   227
edition 9
editorial   1
educate   256, 263
education   18, 94, 135
effect 262

effective   21, 26, 108, 114, 126, 146, 175, 188, 208, 212, 227-230, 238
effects 49, 135, 137, 157
efficiency   64, 98
efficient   47, 82, 138, 215, 220
effort   45, 50, 56, 116, 156, 187, 210, 241
efforts 31, 79, 141, 152
electronic   1, 213
element   156
elements   10, 36, 66, 96, 121, 150, 155-156, 191, 219, 231, 236, 246
elicit   190
eliminate   208, 236
eliminated   152
embarking   29
emerging   59, 91, 238
emphasized   217
employed   257
employee   115, 251
employees   17, 19-20, 70, 108, 121, 126, 187
employers   134
empower   8
enable 72, 201
enablers   122
enabling   229
encourage   86, 90
end-users   205
engage   114, 244
engagement 52, 134, 229
engine 238
enhance   101, 244, 249
enhanced   126
enhancing   97
enlarged   207
enough   8, 65, 111, 115, 117, 147, 179, 206, 211, 244
ensure 32, 39, 66, 79, 103, 110-111, 114, 132, 151, 186-187, 190, 194, 212, 214, 242-243, 265
ensures   110
ensuring   10, 110, 173, 219, 229, 247-248
entered   149
Enterprise   220
entire   193
entities 53

entity   1, 145
equipment   17, 24, 172, 187, 204, 249
equipped   38
equitably   34, 234
equivalent   210
errors   110, 180, 250
essence   236
essential   79, 181
essentials   117, 216
establish   74, 98, 182, 205
estimate   50, 54, 139-140, 158, 175-176, 180-181
-estimate   180
estimated   30, 34, 47, 50, 105, 182-183, 251-252
estimates   4, 38, 48, 64, 139-140, 172, 176, 180, 184, 192, 211, 215
Estimating   4, 174, 178, 182-183
estimation   82
estimator   181
etcetera   50, 114
ethical 17, 126, 254
ethnic 110
European   258
evaluate   76, 86, 155, 212
evaluated   196, 212
evaluating   75, 78
evaluation   78, 89, 96, 212-213, 244, 258
evaluative   219
events 16, 75, 80, 85, 132, 155, 249
everyday   70
everyone   34, 40, 150, 188, 228
everything   52, 226
evidence   11, 45, 135, 189, 202-203, 221, 250
evolution   44
evolve 94
exactly192
examined   41
example   2, 9, 13, 17, 64, 96, 140, 151, 156
examples   8-9, 218
exceed   153, 176
exceeding   52
excellence   8, 34
excellent   45
exciting   236

exclude 76
execute 253
executed 224, 258
Executing 6, 214, 218
execution 98, 129, 140, 152, 187, 219, 222
executive 8, 110, 142
executives 125
exercise 20
existence 209
existing 10, 96, 108, 245
exists 167
expect 112, 143, 174, 178, 206, 212
expected 24, 39, 76, 103, 116, 139-140, 180, 226, 242, 245, 258, 262
expecting 263
expend 50
expense 245-246
expenses 246
experience 38, 114, 118-119, 204, 207, 251
experiment 117
expertise 86, 139, 205, 234, 250
experts 39, 206, 257
expiration 167
explained 10
explicit 191
explicitly 112
explore 66
exposures 77
express 259
extent 11, 21-22, 26, 40, 88, 137-138, 155, 193, 238
external 31, 110, 188, 205
extreme 235
facilitate 11, 17, 68, 99
facilities 228, 230
facility 249
facing 23
fact-based 244
factors 56, 89, 130, 152, 164, 182, 201, 207
failed 50
failure 49, 110, 112
failures 223
fairly 34
familiar 9

fashion 1, 32
feasible   54, 71, 119, 182, 223
feature 10
features   140, 186, 204, 206, 253
feedback   32, 41, 50, 194
filter   188
finalize 212
finalized   13
finally   143
financial   56, 63-64, 70, 107, 116, 136, 187, 200, 203, 258
findings   188
fingertips   10
finish   160, 164-165, 167, 247
finished   164
fiscal   264
focuses   130
follow 98, 124, 126, 138, 166, 253, 256
followed   38, 158, 178, 214, 265
following   9, 11
follow-on   255
for--and   101
forecast   247
forecasts   156
forefront   122
forever 105
forget   10
formal 7, 121, 158, 179, 214, 253-254, 265
formally   33, 130, 151, 184
format 10, 232
formats   200
forming   187
formula   12, 106
Formulate   28
forward   104
foster   104, 123, 195, 202
framework   97, 125, 190-191
freaky 111
frequency   36, 97, 125, 190, 264
frequently   48, 136, 244
friend   112, 116
frontiers   83
fulfill   117
full-blown   46

full-scale 77
fulltime 196
function 150, 254, 257
functional 192, 237
functions 39, 116, 127, 149, 171, 194, 214, 231
funded 255
funding 117-118, 129, 241, 243, 255, 257
further 193, 203
future 8, 54, 92, 97, 109, 155, 245
gained 66, 92, 97, 237
gather 11, 29-30, 33, 35, 38, 44, 60, 67, 71
gathered 32, 63, 66-67, 71-72
gathering 34-35, 43, 145, 204
general 88, 162, 197
generally 220
generate 58-59, 188
generated 67, 129
generation 9, 65
getting 54, 226, 239
Global 79, 135
govern 117
governance 24, 108, 194, 228, 237
governing 198
granted 234
graphics 26
graphs 9
greater 140
greatest 76
ground 70
groups 121, 211, 216, 221, 229, 265
growth 65, 69, 164
guarantee 75
guidance 1
guidelines 226, 257
guides 140
handle 168, 204, 208, 232
handled 204, 213
handling 205, 229
happen 22, 127, 164, 202, 209
happened 130
happens 8, 30, 47, 55, 109, 115, 117, 145, 159, 183, 208-209, 237, 261
hardest 50

hardly 247
hardware   172
havent 118
hazards   208
health 127, 214
healthy   186
hearing   110
helping   8, 150
hidden 46
higher 156
highest 17
high-level   37-38, 132
highlight   194-195, 202
Highly 66
high-tech   124
hijacking   126
hinder 195
hiring 99
historical   182
history 165, 264
hitters 73
hitting 248
honest 126
hoping 133
horizon 107
humans   8
hypotheses   58
identified   1, 18, 23, 26, 36, 40, 59-61, 70, 75, 86, 138, 142,
150-151, 155, 159, 178, 185, 187, 189, 193, 197, 203, 205, 218,
226, 232, 246, 256, 258
identifier   133
identify 10-11, 23-24, 59, 64, 70, 77, 136, 155, 164, 182, 192, 198,
229
identity 236
ignore 27
ignoring   125
images 146
imbedded   92
Immediate   136
impact 5, 31, 45, 48, 50, 52, 54, 56, 84, 120, 129, 135, 146, 185,
204, 206, 213, 224, 237, 239, 241, 265
impacted   53
impacts   48, 53, 175

implement   21, 50, 90, 242
implicit 104
importance   236
important   23, 27, 38, 61-62, 104, 106, 114, 123, 137, 172,
184, 186, 188, 216, 236, 241, 256
improve   2, 10, 72, 74-79, 81-84, 87, 170, 180, 188, 231, 255-
256, 262-263
improved   78, 81, 83, 99, 212
improves   130
improving   220
inadequate   205
incentives   99, 237
include   25, 76, 86, 140, 143, 150, 159, 178, 196, 212-213,
236, 245
included   2, 8, 52, 174, 183, 189, 206, 222, 251-252, 260
INCLUDES   10
including   25, 31, 37, 40, 51, 56, 64, 91, 96, 99, 192, 204
increase   88, 126
increased   195
incurred   44
in-depth   9, 11
indicate   66, 91, 121
indicated   93
indicative   258
indicators   26, 55-56, 61-62, 73, 84, 99, 193, 201
indirect   46, 193, 238, 245-246
indirectly   1
individual   1, 238, 243, 252, 258
industries   204
industry   100, 110, 123, 164, 197, 229, 249
influence   83, 105, 134, 194, 198-199, 226-227, 239, 263
influences   135, 198
informal   243
informed   107, 186, 250
ingrained   95
inherent   108, 195
in-house   132
initial   30, 121, 132
initially 40
initiated   183, 224
initiating   2, 114, 129, 152
initiative   11, 133, 190, 198
Innovate   74

innovation   47, 62, 64, 79, 96, 104, 119, 136
innovative   114, 135, 182
in-process   73
inputs 29, 41, 45, 59, 92, 129
inside 20
insight 58, 71
insights 9
inspect223
inspector   223
inspired   124
instead124, 173
insure   104
integrate   85, 91, 115
integrated   69, 129, 205
integrity   17, 116, 224
intended   1, 79
INTENT 16, 28, 44, 58, 74, 90, 103
intention   1
interact   127
interest121, 188, 208, 214, 221, 265
interests   21, 217
intergroup   236
interim 120
internal   1, 31, 70, 110, 117, 130, 165, 188, 257
interpret   11
intervals   142
interview   122
introduce   202
invariably   258
inventory   181
invest 64
investment   26, 49, 59, 190
investor   54
invitation   258
invoices   158
involve 122, 135, 173, 219
involved   25, 37, 62, 64, 81, 124, 136-137, 150, 193, 198,
220, 241, 260
involves   91
issued 258
issues 18-19, 21, 25-27, 130, 133, 149, 166, 168, 177, 187, 214,
250, 262, 264
iteration   214

iterative   145
itself   1, 19
jointly   243
judgment   1
justified99, 187, 258
killer   114
knowledge   10, 29, 31, 38, 66, 83, 86, 92-93, 97, 99-101, 106,
113, 123, 125, 216, 237, 260
labeled   193
lacked 100
languages   233
largely 64
latest 9
leader 21, 69, 84
leaders40, 65, 100, 111, 120, 198, 211, 250
leadership   20, 31, 35, 79, 111, 127, 136
learned   7, 97, 126, 253, 255, 263-264
learning   93, 96, 101, 227, 238
legally 229
length 233
lesson 255, 263
lessons 7, 77, 97, 126, 253, 264
levels 17, 25, 39, 61-62, 84, 97, 100, 127, 136, 153, 187
leverage   42, 79, 97, 118, 174, 182
leveraged   31
leveraging   238
liability 1
licensed   1
licenses   155
lifecycle   55, 73
lifecycles   86
Lifetime   10
likelihood   79, 84
likely   80, 92, 116, 136, 200-201, 227
limitation   54
limited 10, 194
linear 145
linked 41
listed   1, 177, 191
listen   108, 115, 234
loaded212
locally 80
location   233

logged222
logical 155, 168
longer 97
long-term   99, 111
looking20, 241, 249
losing 54
losses 24, 31
lowest 156, 166
magnitude   88
maintain   90, 116, 130, 186
maintained   87, 193
makers81, 130, 218
making   21, 62, 76, 84, 120, 141, 190-191
manage   38, 40, 45, 53, 55, 72, 78-79, 87, 89, 125, 127, 130, 132-133, 147, 162, 184, 190, 200, 239-240, 250
manageable 42, 75, 210
managed   8, 30, 65, 67, 69, 78, 80, 82, 85, 98, 100, 205, 211, 222, 254, 264
Management 1-7, 9-14, 16-43, 45-57, 59-145, 147, 149-153, 155-156, 158-168, 170-188, 190, 192-200, 202-208, 210-212, 214-222, 224-229, 231-233, 235, 237, 239, 241-243, 245-251, 253-258, 260-262, 264-265
manager   8, 10, 20, 30, 32, 107, 130, 132, 178, 212, 214, 220, 254, 264
managers   2, 128, 139, 159, 204, 210, 218-219, 249
manages   77, 133, 251
managing   2, 78, 128, 134, 176, 205, 228, 262
Mandated   206
mandatory   224, 262
manner   24, 76, 215, 218, 223, 244-245, 254, 256
manpower   156
mantle116
manual   152
Mapping   62, 68-69
market 17, 164, 201, 236, 245, 248, 257
marketable   201
marketer   8
Marketing   105, 164, 263
markets   24
master 155
material   156, 164, 188, 192
materials   1
matrices   147

Matrix 3, 5, 135, 147, 192, 206
matter 39, 55-56
mattered   265
matters   226
maximize   238
meaning   162
meaningful   104, 156, 193, 238
measurable   32, 42, 258
measure   2, 10, 18, 38, 42, 44, 46-49, 51-52, 55, 64, 74-75,
78, 84-86, 93-96, 98, 132, 136, 182, 185, 188-189, 235
measured   22, 45, 49-53, 56, 81, 92, 96, 186, 208, 249
measures   45, 48, 51, 55-56, 61-62, 64, 73, 84, 91, 99-100,
138, 187-188, 191, 208, 222, 237, 243
measuring   97, 193, 245
mechanical   1
mechanics   222
mechanism   152, 205, 263
mediated   234
medium   247
meeting   31, 35, 91, 130, 141, 184, 191, 194, 220, 230-231,
233-234
meetings   29, 40, 43, 130, 218, 226, 233
megatrends   109
member   6, 35, 122, 127, 171, 220, 233, 237
members   30-32, 34, 67, 90, 149-150, 176, 178, 196, 198, 231,
233-236, 238, 240, 243-244, 249, 264
membership   236
memorable   188, 238
mentors   249
message   101, 216-217
messages   198, 233
method   47, 140, 174, 198, 236
methods   32, 36, 54, 71, 142, 159, 182, 186, 233
metrics 4, 42, 63, 99, 143, 188, 200
milestone   4, 132, 141, 159, 164, 167, 173, 178, 184, 196
milestones   37, 134, 156, 158, 167
minimal   236
minimize   129, 177, 200
minimizing   73
minimum   251
minority   21
minutes   31, 74, 141, 231
missed 53, 110

missing 63, 112, 163
mission 67, 71, 106, 115, 196, 258
mitigate 79, 129, 150
mitigated 256
mitigation 140, 177, 179
mix-ups 229
mobile 238
Modeling 64, 190
models 17, 52, 71, 125
modified 98
modifier 189
module 143
moment 103
moments 59
momentum 110, 121
monetary 21, 242
monitor 93-95, 99, 182, 257
monitored 90, 98, 175
monitoring 6, 92-94, 97-99, 144, 168, 201, 222, 241
months 74, 80
Morale 136
motivate 121
motivation 27, 101
motive 190
moving 104
multiple 211
narrow 58
native 233
nature 192
nearest 12
nearly 105
necessary 59, 71-72, 81, 114, 125-126, 142, 182, 201, 213, 218, 225, 232, 237, 257-258
needed 17-18, 20-22, 27, 29, 59-60, 65, 93-94, 97, 145, 172, 179, 183, 191, 218, 264
negative 105
negatively 202, 218
negotiate 118
negotiated 107
neither 1
network 4, 166-167, 176, 243
Neutral 11, 16, 28, 44, 58, 74, 90, 103
normal 95, 173

Notice 1
noticing   226
notified   213, 216, 260
notify   233
number   27, 43, 51, 57, 73, 89, 102, 127, 162, 172, 250, 257, 266
numbers   115
numerous   260-261
objection   17
objective   8, 46, 136, 180
objectives   18-19, 23, 28, 41, 67, 71, 91, 107-108, 121, 137, 145, 159, 173, 178-179, 197, 202, 220, 237-238, 262
obligates   172
observe   194
observed   77
observing   152
obsolete   109
obstacles   23, 182
obtain 115, 254
obtained   41, 142
obtaining   45
obvious   236
obviously   11
occurred   202
occurrence   223
occurring   76
occurs 50, 94, 229, 256
offerings   62, 85
offerors212
office   196, 210, 220, 260
officials261
offsite 206
one-time   8
ongoing   86, 92, 175
opened   246
operates   123
operating   6, 53, 55, 94, 138, 155, 184, 233
operation   98, 175, 241
operations   10, 91, 95, 97, 99, 184, 229
operators   98, 249
opponent   227
opponents   239
opposite   123

optimal   83, 212, 251
optimize   83, 97
optimized   114
option 119
options20, 181, 203
orderly 229
orders 258-259
organized   162
orient 91
oriented   158
original176, 228
originally   152
originate   199
others 182-183, 193, 198-199, 201, 227-228, 235, 256, 259, 263
otherwise   1, 185
outcome   11, 75, 130, 133, 258
outcomes   84, 97, 122, 135, 182, 248-250, 262
outlined   91
output 42, 59, 61-63, 65, 67, 71, 91, 95
outputs   41, 59, 63, 69, 92, 168
outside86, 173, 218-219
outsource   61, 172, 261
outsourced   219
outweigh   45
overall 10-11, 19, 55, 91, 107, 127, 137, 145, 177, 202, 226, 234, 241, 252, 256
overcome   182
overhead   155-156, 192, 245-246
overlook   240
overlooked   219, 255
overseas   204
oversees   130
oversight   60, 196, 210
overtime   168
owners 154
ownership   37, 100
package   155, 245
packages   155-156
paradigms   120
paragraph   108
parallel   166
parameters   100
Pareto 73

particular   64, 241
Parties 77, 260
partners   25, 37, 77, 95, 111, 115, 121, 138, 164, 204
pathways   69
pattern   162
patterns   83
paycheck   122
paying 115
payment   158, 211, 260
payments   197
pending   225
people8, 18, 45, 51, 60, 72, 81, 85, 90, 101, 104-105, 108-110,
112, 114, 117-118, 124, 126-127, 172, 191-193, 197, 200, 206-208,
214-217, 221, 248, 250
perceive   114
percent   123
percentage   147
perception   77-78, 126
perform   18, 32, 34, 37, 171, 208, 223, 253
performed   86, 147, 160-161, 173, 180, 193, 201, 203, 231
performing   129, 212
perhaps   17, 248
period 88, 192, 202, 237
periodic   210
permission   1
person 1, 20, 181, 192
personal   105
personally   147
personnel   21, 23, 68, 98, 167, 176, 179, 190, 204, 211
pertaining   204
pertinent   98
phases 55, 86, 130, 198, 255
pieces 214
pitfalls 108, 265
places 213
planet 101
planned   91, 95-96, 98, 143, 155, 163, 175, 193, 202, 262-
263
planning   3, 9, 91, 94, 137, 143, 150, 156, 166, 168, 170, 221,
228-229, 241, 245, 249
platform   238
platforms   237-238
players 81

pocket 182
pockets   182
points 27, 43, 57, 61, 73, 89, 101, 127, 190
policies   141, 204, 216, 249
policy 83, 132, 168, 265
political   113, 138, 198, 207, 239
population   137
portfolio   111
portray 73
position   194
positioned   182
positive   80, 105, 110, 139-140, 229, 236
positively   202
possible   50, 58-59, 85, 90, 119, 174, 196, 237
posted 249
potential   24, 56, 66, 75-76, 109, 112, 122, 150, 155, 203,
209, 214, 241
practical   71, 74, 83, 90, 221
practiced   129
practices   1, 10, 73, 83, 97, 99, 195, 217-218, 237-238, 253
precaution   1
precede   166
predict 222
predicting   97
Prediction   162, 202
predictors   223
preferred   263
pre-filled   9
prepare   190, 195
prepared   213
preparing   258
present   97, 109, 112, 143, 205, 207
presented   27, 232
presenting   228
preserve   29
preserved   63
prevent   46, 229, 234
prevented   229
preventive   208
prevents   21
previous   31, 129, 251, 255
previously   224
prices 212

primary 170
priorities 45, 48, 50-51, 55
prioritize 192
priority 50, 54, 236
privacy 30, 140
probably 170
problem 16-17, 19-21, 24, 27-28, 31-32, 37, 40, 45, 54, 66, 71, 145, 214, 221, 244, 247
problems 18-19, 21, 23, 25-26, 76, 80, 82, 93, 108, 138, 191, 265
procedure 157, 229, 233
procedures 10, 78, 94, 98, 168, 181, 184, 216, 226, 245, 257-258
proceeding 175-176
process 1-4, 6-8, 10, 29, 34, 37-38, 41-42, 59-72, 77, 80, 91, 93-97, 99-100, 129-130, 132, 137, 141, 144-145, 147-152, 168, 174, 179-180, 186-187, 190-191, 195, 200, 204, 206-207, 214, 218, 231, 241, 247-248, 250-251, 255, 262
processes 55, 61, 64, 67-73, 96, 99, 129, 131, 138, 190, 200, 216, 218, 224, 228, 245, 253, 255-256, 264
produce 65, 129, 168, 221
produced 67, 80
producing 147
product 1, 50, 61-62, 114, 116, 143, 150, 164, 176, 184, 186, 188, 201, 208, 218, 220-221, 225, 231, 247-248, 254-255
production 33, 86
products 1, 17, 25, 45, 110-111, 147, 156, 204, 218, 220, 225, 243, 264
profile 229
profit 188
program 46, 60, 94, 131, 139, 202, 242
programs 221, 228, 249
progress 39, 52, 86, 91, 120, 126, 132, 138, 156, 182, 190-191, 196-197, 235, 264
prohibited 157
project 2-4, 6-9, 18-19, 24, 43, 46, 72-73, 83, 91, 95, 98, 104-105, 107, 109, 112-113, 116, 118, 121-122, 128-130, 132-145, 147, 149-154, 156, 158-161, 163, 165-167, 170-185, 187, 192-193, 195-198, 202-205, 207, 210-212, 214-215, 217-221, 224-225, 231-232, 239, 241-243, 247, 250-251, 253-256, 258, 260, 262, 264-265
projects 2, 55, 108-109, 123, 128, 131, 135-138, 147, 150, 153, 159, 172-173, 177, 194, 205-206, 210-211, 219-221, 247-248, 262

promising   114
promote   45, 60, 136
promotion   195
proofing   77
proper 93, 186, 211
properly   33, 40, 146, 157, 222, 228, 258
proponents   239
proposal   212
proposed   21, 47, 50, 139-140, 143, 145, 203, 212, 214, 251-
252, 259
protect   72, 104, 140
protected   63
protection   200
proved253
provide   71, 114, 118, 134, 140, 155-156, 167, 180-182, 189,
196, 218, 243-244
provided   12, 91, 136, 151, 187, 213-214, 264
providers   77, 211
provides   170, 210
providing   93, 134, 185
provision   227
published   258
publisher   1
pulled 123
purchase   8, 172, 210, 231, 258-259
purchases   214
purpose   2, 10, 115, 136, 150, 170, 183, 190, 233, 235-236,
238, 243
purposes   155
pushing   111
qualified   34, 60, 62, 66-67, 70, 215, 249
qualifies   61, 65
qualify 53, 59, 65
qualities   20
quality 1, 4, 6, 10, 23, 45-46, 52, 60, 63-64, 68-69, 85, 95, 100, 130,
142, 159, 172, 176-177, 186-191, 194, 213, 218, 226, 228-231, 242,
250, 264
quantified   92
quantify   53
quarterly   246
question   11, 16, 28, 44, 58, 74, 90, 103, 116, 190
questions   8-9, 11, 71, 175, 219, 240
quickly 10, 64, 192

quotes 212
radically   72
raised 214
rather 107
Rating 237
rational   245
rationale   179, 226, 246
reached   17
reaching   108
reactivate   124
readiness   33, 197
readings   93
realistic   17, 66, 110, 139, 205-206
realized   120
really   8, 21, 42
reason 113, 123, 217
reasonable   75, 112, 140, 211, 215, 257
reasons   29
rebuild 114
receipt 229
receive   9-10, 30, 46, 217, 232
received   39, 124, 201, 213, 257
receives   237
recently   110
recipient   22, 261
recognised   80
recognize   2, 16-17, 20-21, 25-26, 77, 83, 88
recognized   17, 20-22, 24, 26, 65, 197, 239
recognizes   20
recommend   116, 198
record 233
recorded   186
recording   1, 233-234
records   59, 125, 187, 193, 260
Recovery   202
recruit 187
recurrence   209
redefine   17, 36
re-define   235
re-design   71
reduce 45, 53, 138, 227, 236
reduced   208
reducing   91, 205

references   266
reflect 66, 94, 100, 151, 156-157
reform 44, 103, 119, 138
reforms21, 50, 54
regarding   105-106, 152, 181, 186, 213, 220
Register   2, 5, 134, 202-203
regular 39-40, 65, 251
regularly   29-30, 130, 172, 184, 218
regulatory   26
reinforced   138
relate 67, 107, 224
related17, 51, 61, 95, 131, 187, 194, 198, 222-223, 246-247
relation   19, 24, 85, 115, 135
relations   110, 202
relative91, 236
relatively   121
release158, 198, 214
releases   252
Relevance   257
relevant   32, 53, 71, 97, 120, 142, 149, 152, 159, 234
reliable38, 215
remain 35
remaining   177, 183
remember   174
remove   208
repair 197
repeat 129
rephrased   10
replace   48
replaced   138
replicated   255
report 6-7, 79, 93, 141, 196, 220, 231, 243, 251, 258
reported   192, 247
reporting   71, 93, 127, 144, 156, 186, 200, 249
reports 46, 134, 139, 144, 264
repository   158, 211
represent   81, 225
reproduced   1
reputation   107
request   6, 71, 196, 222-225
requested   1, 76, 130, 225
requests   222
require 46, 61, 73, 96, 98, 168, 243

required 17, 21, 29-30, 33-34, 38, 42, 68, 79, 87, 100, 129,
155, 161-162, 174, 198, 216, 257, 262
requiring 134, 260
research 17, 113-114, 228
resemble 173
reserved 1
reserves 136, 193, 196
reside 88, 180, 211, 233
resolution 71, 80, 234
resolve 19, 21, 236
resolved 215, 234
Resource 4-5, 109, 129, 156, 162, 168, 170, 173, 196, 221
resources 2, 8, 19, 22-23, 28, 32, 38, 50, 62, 79, 94, 100, 105,
109-110, 130, 135, 139, 141, 143, 145, 151, 161-162, 167, 170, 172,
174, 176, 182, 187, 214, 232, 237, 241, 243
respect 1
respond 138
responded 12
responding 203
response 17, 91-93, 98, 101, 213, 251
responses 87, 105
responsive 183
restrict 145
result 70, 80-81, 180, 183, 225, 235, 261
resulted 99, 238
resulting 70, 137, 140, 149
results 9, 29, 39, 62, 74-77, 79, 82, 84-85, 88, 91, 99, 139, 162,
173, 176, 183, 186, 188, 249-250, 253, 258
retain 103, 187
retained 69
retention 53
retrospect 123
return 80, 116, 166, 190, 258
returns 136
revealed 259
revenue 26, 51
review 10, 33, 64, 139, 176-178, 180, 227
reviewed 37, 129, 142, 151, 173, 230, 258
reviewer 236
reviews 141, 167, 172, 178, 196, 206, 211, 214
revised 64, 99, 230
revisions 260
revisit 226

reward 45, 61, 221
rewarded   17
rewards   99
rework 54, 57
rights   1
robustness   135
routine 92
safely   208
Safety 1-14, 16-43, 45-54, 56-57, 59, 61-145, 147, 149-153,
155-156, 158-168, 170-188, 190, 192-198, 200, 202-208, 210-212,
214-222, 224-226, 228, 231-233, 235, 237, 239, 241-243, 245-251,
253-258, 260, 262, 264-265
Sampling   186
satisfied   112, 253-254
satisfies 247
satisfying   114
savings 38, 55, 64
scalable   85
scenario   31, 40
schedule   3-4, 35, 52, 92, 119, 142, 155, 158-159, 166-167,
176-178, 184, 193, 196, 200, 210-211, 225, 232, 245, 252
scheduled   156, 196, 218
scheduler   178
schedules   155, 176-177
scheduling   155-158, 197
scheme   101
Science   60, 174
scientific   174
Scorecard   2, 12-14, 219
scorecards   99
Scores 14
scoring 10
screening   140, 189
seamless   104
second   12
section 12, 27, 43, 57, 73, 89, 101-102, 127
sector 248
securing   52, 111
security   18, 69-70, 87, 95, 134, 186, 188, 224
segmented   40
segments   29, 121, 245-246
select 60, 91
selected   88, 140, 182, 205-206, 216

selecting   70, 108, 140, 233
selection   5, 212, 258
seller   172, 213
sellers   1
selling   117, 227
senior   100, 104, 111, 127
sensitive   31, 56, 138
sequence   155, 161
sequencing   119
series   11
service 1-2, 8, 50, 77-78, 100, 114, 164, 184, 186, 201, 220-221
services   1, 45, 47, 51, 111, 114, 120, 181, 213, 219, 230,
233, 245-246, 251, 254, 261
session 143
setting 110, 117
Several72, 206
severely   71
Severity   202
shared 97, 183, 226, 245
sharing83, 101, 243, 246
shifts   25
short-term   235
should 8, 16, 19, 21, 23, 30, 32, 34, 38, 46, 49, 55, 60, 64-65, 68-
69, 80-81, 87, 95, 98, 108-109, 121, 124-125, 127, 129, 134, 138,
140, 143-144, 152, 160, 162, 173, 175, 180, 184, 189-190, 194-195,
200, 202-203, 205-206, 208, 213, 217-218, 224, 231-232, 237, 249,
257
sigmas 130
signature   111
signatures   168
signed 149
signers 261
similar 31, 43, 62, 73, 85, 162, 165, 198, 211
simple 121, 192, 248
simply 9, 227
single   108, 156, 258
single-use   8
situation   22, 44, 180, 203, 207, 247
situations   101, 235
skeptical   105
skills   24-25, 106, 123, 196, 207, 235, 237-238, 244, 255
smaller 137
smallest   24, 80

smoothly   217
social 105, 230, 236
societal   117
software   17, 129, 143, 146, 155, 172-173, 177, 205, 212, 218, 252
solicit 32
solution   46, 71, 74, 77, 79, 81-85, 88-90, 251
solutions   46, 75-77, 82, 92, 258
solved 21
solving 244
someone   8, 258
someones   236
something   105
Sometimes   46
sought 136
source 5, 103, 118, 180, 212
sources   38, 66, 73, 146, 206, 215
special 29, 91, 133
specific   9, 19, 32, 42, 59, 126, 151, 160, 168, 180, 194, 204, 206, 212, 214, 221, 224, 235, 258
specified   108, 156, 159, 255
specify 243
spoken 110
sponsor   23, 132, 150, 179, 197, 254
sponsors   25, 218, 231
spread 96, 101
stability 150, 189
staffed 32
staffing 25, 99
staffs   237
stages 229
standard   8, 94, 100, 129, 168, 251-252
standards   1, 10-11, 92, 95, 99-100, 151, 186, 188, 191, 215, 224
started 9, 164, 166
starting 10
startup 132
stated 108, 112, 187, 194, 233, 257
statement   3, 11, 80, 82, 149-151, 180
statements   12, 27, 32, 37, 43, 57, 66, 73, 89, 102, 127, 190
static   222
status 6-7, 60, 135, 142, 156, 159, 172, 193, 196-197, 200, 210, 220, 222, 231, 240, 247, 251

steady 47
Steering   142, 152
storage   229
stories 33
strategic   50, 86, 91, 133, 159, 178, 197, 229
strategies   83, 94, 103, 137, 177, 226-227, 238
strategy   19, 37, 56, 74-75, 99, 105, 107, 118, 122, 125, 151, 198, 226, 245, 262
Stream 68-69
strengths   152, 164, 212, 253
stretch 117
strict   70
strictly 258
strive   117, 218
strong 194
Strongly   11, 16, 28, 44, 58, 74, 90, 103, 223
structure   3-4, 83, 108, 121, 153-154, 170, 205, 212, 216
structured   112, 210
stubborn   118
stupid 111
subdivided   155
subject 9-10, 39, 143
subjects   66
submitted   224
subset 24
sub-teams   237
succeed   47, 115, 164, 235
success   18, 22, 31, 33, 37-38, 46, 48-49, 51, 78, 84-86, 96, 106, 111, 114, 116, 121, 126, 137, 151, 179-180, 187, 201, 210, 214, 220, 227, 241, 255-256, 262, 265
successes   106
successful   65, 79, 83, 98, 107, 109, 115, 130, 170-171, 184-185, 218-220
succession   101, 135
sufficient   138, 205, 237, 241
suggest   201, 223, 229
suggested   93, 224-225
suitable   206
supervisor   194
supplier   77, 127, 204
suppliers   41, 69-70, 111, 179, 229
supplies   253
supply 47, 135, 217

support 8, 22, 62, 81, 95, 97, 104, 114, 130, 136, 155, 168, 197, 226, 251
supported 64, 206
supporting 87, 93
supports 130
supposed 228
surface 93
SUSTAIN 2, 84, 103
sustained 242
Sustaining 99, 165
symptom 16, 46
system 10, 34, 70-71, 96, 111, 118, 145-146, 151, 156, 170, 211, 224, 226, 228-229, 245, 247-248
systematic 49, 245
Systems 1-7, 9-14, 16-43, 45-54, 56-57, 59-145, 147, 149-153, 155-156, 158-168, 170-188, 190, 192-198, 200, 202-208, 210-212, 214-222, 224-226, 228-229, 231-233, 235, 237-239, 241-243, 245-251, 253-258, 260, 262, 264-265
tackle 46
tactics 226-227
taking 51, 130, 137, 221
talent 60, 127
talents 123
talking 8
tallied 184
tangible 250
target 41, 137, 238
targets 117, 132, 248
tasked 100
teaming 234
technical 86, 129, 139, 145, 156, 213
technique 219
techniques 71, 125, 158
technology 48, 82, 100, 114, 136-137, 145, 164, 204-205, 233
templates 8-9
tender 257-258
tendering 258
tenders 257-258
testable 36
test-cycle 191
tested 25
testing 75, 145, 155, 206, 249-250
themes 238

themselves   112, 235
theory 101
therein 246
things 75, 122, 180, 188, 200, 218, 241, 255, 265
thinking   70, 86, 119
third- 77
thorough   85, 224
thought   198
threat 20, 109, 236
threats 209
through   63, 65, 111, 149, 200, 238, 250
throughout   1, 73, 109, 152, 167
tighter 105
time-based   155
time-bound   32
timeframe   58, 163, 182
timeframes   21
timeline   158, 225, 242
timeliness   186
timely 24, 32, 76, 215, 218, 223, 256, 264
timing 206
together   114, 192, 264
tolerances   75, 239
tolerated   160
tomorrow   101, 122
top-down   97
topics 86
toward91, 221
towards   71, 138
traceable   245
traced 185
tracked   149, 158-159
tracking   33, 91, 144, 179, 197
traction   106
trademark   1
trademarks   1
tradeoff   213
trained 40, 204, 249
training   18, 21, 26, 68, 71, 86, 91, 94, 99, 201, 216, 218,
220, 237-238
trainings   27
Transfer   12, 27, 43, 57, 73, 89, 99-100, 102, 127, 251
transition   201

translated   42
trends   59, 61-62, 84, 114, 139-140, 187
trigger   75, 88
triggered   159
triggers 77, 141
trophy   116
trouble 116
trying   8, 113, 126, 188, 228, 230
turnaround   163
two-page   172
unable 233
uncover   193
uncovered   145
underlying   82
undermine   113
understand   35, 68, 129, 144, 238, 249
understood   75, 124, 146, 235
undertake   72, 203
underway   76
uninformed   107
unique 106, 135
Unless   8
unpriced   192
unresolved   158, 168
update   177, 263
updated   9-10, 66, 173, 210, 222
updates   10, 99, 200, 251
updating   179, 214
urgent 222
usability   78, 119
useful   82, 95, 153, 201
usefully 10, 24
utility   175
utilized 238
utilizing 84
validate   54, 248
validated   37-38, 62, 67, 129
Validation   248
validity 242
valuable   8
values   100, 111, 195-196, 208
variables   61, 95, 227
variance   6, 236, 245

-variance 178
variances 155
variation 16, 39, 66, 73, 91
variety 85
vendor 84, 129, 158, 167, 258
vendors 25, 70, 77, 149, 179
verified 10, 37-38, 67, 129
verify 45, 49-54, 56, 96-98, 177, 238, 247, 257, 260
version 252, 266
versions 29, 34
versus 143
vested 121, 208
viable 92, 153
violated 152
Violation 152
Virtual 234
vis-à-vis 205
vision 111, 139-140, 196
visual 188
visualize 160
voices 134
volatile 79
volatility 200
volume 156
volunteers 233
warning 159
warranty 1
weaknesses 142, 212, 253
weekly 130
whether 8, 91, 121, 194, 237
widespread 91
willing 204-206
window 163
withheld 257
within 72, 88, 162, 175, 185, 192, 204, 220, 224, 254
without 1, 12, 114, 146, 224, 259-260
worked 140, 197-198, 241
workers 110
workflow 62, 227
workforce 25, 84, 111, 114, 121
working 91, 96, 176, 214, 226
workload 200
Worksheet 4, 174, 182

worksheets   212
worried   236
worst-case   31
writing 147
written 1, 229
youhave   143
yourself   110, 122, 126, 149, 195

Made in the USA
Columbia, SC
11 April 2024

34219047R00186